Said Nursi

MAKERS OF ISLAMIC CIVILIZATION

Series editor: Farhan A. Nizami

This series, conceived by the Oxford Centre for Islamic Studies, is jointly published by Oxford University Press and I.B. Tauris. The books in the series, written by leading scholars in the field, aim to provide an introduction to outstanding figures in the history of Islamic civilization. They will serve as the essential first point of reference for study of the persons, events and ideas that have shaped the Islamic world and the cultural resources on which Muslims continue to draw.

Said Nursi

Colin Turner
Hasan Horkuc

Oxford Centre for Islamic Studies

Published in 2009 by I.B. Tauris & Co. Ltd. and Oxford University Press India
in association with the Oxford Centre for Islamic Studies

I.B.Tauris & Co. Ltd.
6 Salem Road, London W2 4BU
175 Fifth Avenue, New York NY 10010
www.ibtauris.com

Distributed in the United States and Canada Exclusively by Palgrave Macmillan
175 Fifth Avenue, New York NY 10010

ISBN 978 1 84511 774 0

For all territories except South Asia

A full CIP record for this book is available from the British Library
A full CIP record is available from the Library of Congress

Library of Congress Catalog Card Number: available

Cover: tile image adapted from photo by Yahya Michot
Typeset in Garamond 11.5/13.8
Printed in India by De-Unique, New Delhi 110 018

Contents

List of maps

* Cartography by Alexander Kent, PhD., FBCart.S., FRGS.

1

Introduction

The Iranian scholar Muhammad Shabistari observes that the numerous movements of the past 150 years, characterized almost without exception as 'Islamic movements', have had little if anything to do with the resurgence of religious faith as such; most have actually been political movements, whose leaders were trying to address the problem of the perceived backwardness of the Muslim peoples and their subservience, politically and culturally, to the West (Shabistari, *Dīn wa āzādī*, 122).

While none of the groups that operate under the loose-fit label of 'Islamic movements' can claim to be identifiable primarily as a faith movement, various individuals have appeared sporadically with the avowed aim of fostering renewal of belief – often to the extent of dedicating their whole life's work to that aim. Around some of these individuals, movements of considerable size and import have accreted. Said Nursi is one such individual.

To say that Nursi stands like a colossus above twentieth-century Muslim scholarship in Turkey is no overstatement. And, as with all intellectual heavyweights in the arena of religious thought, it is no surprise that opinions on him are divided – sometimes starkly so. For some of his disciples and admirers, who number now in their millions, Said Nursi was the 'renewer' (*mujaddid*) of the fourteenth century AH – the most recent in a long line of 'renewers' who, according to a Prophetic tradition, would appear at the beginning of each century to revive Islam and interpret the tenets of the Qur'an in accordance with the understanding and demands of the day. Thus did he earn for himself the honorific 'Bediüzzaman' or 'nonpareil of the age' (Mardin, *Religion and Social Change*, 23). As such he was deemed to be the saviour of an Islam in Turkey that had been ravaged by the onslaught of atheistic materialism and Kemalist nationalism; the most proficient Turkish Muslim theologian and exegete in the modern era; and the founder of the most influential text-based faith community – Nurculuk – in Turkish history.

For many of his detractors, however, there is far more to Nursi than meets the eye. To some he was a hypocrite and a liar, and one whose life was full of contradictions; to others a Kurd in the pay of Communists and an overt proponent of anarchy. He is reviled for his opposition to the secularist reforms of the republic, for his involvement in reactionary activities, and for the fact that he possessed little in the way of formal – meaning secular – education. Despite this polarity of opinion, both supporters and detractors alike would no doubt agree that Nursi is arguably the most important and influential Muslim scholar to emerge from Turkey in the past five hundred years.

Yet almost half a century after his death, Nursi continues to defy attempts to locate him precisely within the generally accepted milieu of 'Muslim scholars'. While his *magnum opus*, the *Risale-i Nur*, is for all intents and purposes a commentary on the Qur'an, it is not a work of exegesis in the technical sense of the word, though he was clearly an accomplished exegete. And while Nursi was well-versed in the principles of *kalām* and the methods of the *mutakallimūn*, and devotes the lion's share of the *Risale* to what he claims are rational proofs for the unity (*tawḥīd*) of God, it is not a work of traditional theology either.

In fact, on one level, the *Risale* is as resistant to compartmentalization as the Qur'an itself, which it claims to mirror and to elucidate. And if, as Nursi often asserts, the aim of the Qur'an is to guide man to belief, then the teachings of the *Risale* should be seen as consonant with that aim.

> The three supreme matters in the worlds of humanity and Islam are belief, the Shari'a, and life. Since the truths of belief are the greatest of these, the Risale-i Nur's select and loyal students avoid politics with abhorrence so that they should not be made the tool for other currents and subject to other forces, and those diamond-like Qur'anic truths not reduced to fragments of glass in the view of those who sell or exploit religion for the world, and so that they can carry out to the letter the duty of saving belief, the greatest duty. (Vahide, 'The Book of the Universe', 261)

Part of Nursi's appeal lay in his uncompromising belief that it is belief (*īmān*) which must be renewed and protected, and that all other endeavours must be approached with the primacy of belief in mind: the fact that, unlike many of the popular Muslim thinkers of his own epoch, he repudiated the dubious art of politics – and, more importantly, the dubious art of politicking that is buttressed by religion – earned him respect and conferred on him a sense of authenticity that would perhaps be found wanting in so many other Muslim thinkers. Another part of his appeal lay in his shrewd interpretation of the forces ranged against him. For Nursi, unlike many of the Muslim scholars, leaders and ideologues who came later, realized that if there is a conflict between Islam – or belief – and modernity, it is not a conflict fought over issues of government or technology, over science or democracy. As Nursi's own evaluation of the problems facing the Muslim world shows, the conflict is ultimately over transcendence, with the post-Enlightenment experiment claiming a centrality in the universe's affairs for man that Islam, with its emphasis on the dependence of man on God, cannot countenance. Man is faced with a choice: belief in the sovereignty of God or belief in the sovereignty of man, with all that such a choice entails. For Nursi, the way to salvation consists solely in choosing the Other over the self, and it is in the dynamics of this choice that the key to an understanding of Nursi's world-view may be found.

2

Life and works

THE FIRST PERIOD: THE 'OLD SAID' 1876–1899

Said Nursi was born in the small village of Nurs, in the province of Bitlis in eastern Turkey. While different dates for his birth are given in the various sources, general consensus has it that he was born in 1293 according to the Rumi calendar then in use in the Ottoman Empire, equivalent to 1876.

Nursi was born into a Kurdish family of seven children, headed by his father, a village mullah named Mirza and his mother, Nuriye. Nursi was their fourth child; all his brothers and sisters – save for his youngest brother, Abdülmecid – predeceased him. While there are reports that he himself claimed that he was descended from the Prophet through both of his parents, there is no official record of his family being *sayyids*.

Nursi spent his early life with his family in Nurs, beginning his education at the age of nine. Owing to the fact that Nurs was a very small village with no school, Nursi was forced to leave his family for the village of Tag and the *medrese* of Molla Mehmed Emin Efendi. However, he was not to stay there long and, following a fight with another student, Nursi went to the village of Pirmir to continue his studies full-time, later studying under the Naqshbandi Seyyid Nur Muhammad Efendi, grandson of the second person in the chain of authorized successors of Mevlana Khalid. After a spell in this *medrese*, Nursi went to the village of Nurşin with his elder brother, Abdullah. In the winter of that year, which Nursi spent in his home village of Nurs, he saw the Prophet in a dream. Inspired by this vision and filled with a renewed desire for education, he decided to leave Nurs once more. In 1888, Nursi set off for the village of Arvas and from there to the *medrese* of Shaykh Emin Efendi in Bitlis.

Again, his unsettled personality meant that he was not destined to stay long in Bitlis, and before long he had moved to the Mir Hasan Veli *medrese* at Müküş, whose principal was Molla Abdülkerim. Unhappy with the fact that the new, lower grade students were accorded no importance, Nursi left for Vastan (Gevaş), near Van. After a month there, he set off for Doğubayazit, a small town in the province of Erzurum. Up until this point, his nomadic existence meant that he had studied nothing more than the principles of Arabic grammar and syntax. According to Şahiner (*Kronolojik Hayatı*, 59), it was in Doğubayazit that his real education began.

At the beginning of his studies in his new school, Nursi received a three month full-time course under the supervision of Shaykh Mehmed Jalali, with whom he studied all the texts being taught in the *medrese*s at that time, albeit rather superficially. When asked about this by his master he replied:

> I am not able to read and comprehend all these books. But I know that they are caskets of jewels: treasure chests, the key to which is in your possession. What I need is a clue to the contents. When I know what topics these texts cover, I will then choose those which are appropriate to my character. (Şahiner, *Kronolojik Hayatı*, 60; see also Mardin, *Religion and Social Change*, 68)

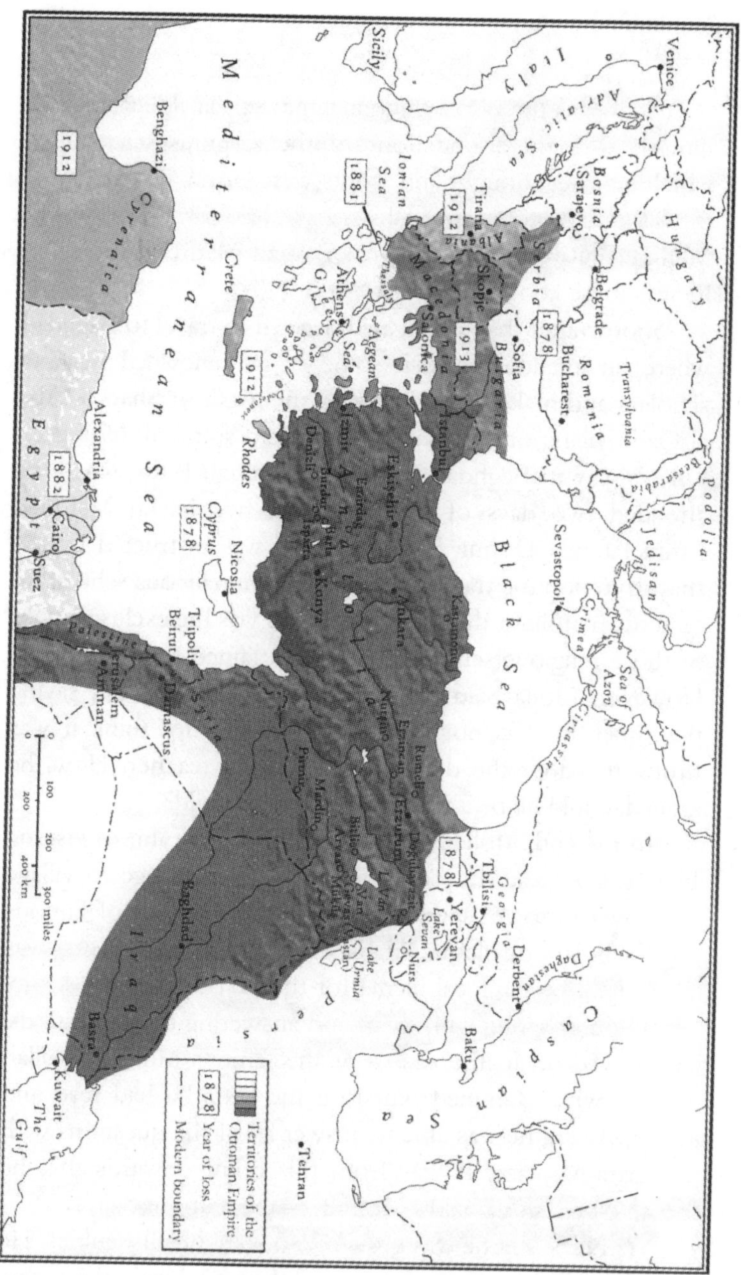

The Ottoman Empire 1878–1922

Yet, in this three-month course, Nursi was able to provide himself with the foundations of the religious sciences on which his later thought and works were based. At the end of the course, Nursi received his *icazet* (diploma) from Shaykh Mehmed Jalali, the Principal of Bayazit Medrese; thereafter he was to be known as 'Molla Said'.

Shortly after that, Molla Said decided to travel to Baghdad, where he intended to visit some of its renowned religious scholars and make a pilgrimage to the tomb of Shaykh 'Abd al-Qadir Jilani, one of Nursi's two main spiritual influences. On his way to Baghdad, he passed through Bitlis, where he attended two days of lectures given by Shaykh Mehmed Emin Efendi. During his stay, Nursi was instructed by the shaykh to don the traditional dress of the religious scholar: in eastern Anatolia at that time the turban was the exclusive right of those religious scholars who had attained their diplomas. However, Molla Said rejected the shaykh's request, saying that since he was not yet mature, he did not think it was fitting to adopt the dress of a respected teacher. How, he argued, could he be a teacher while still a child?

In the end, Molla Said never achieved his aim of visiting Baghdad. Instead, he began to move from village to village and town to town, spending time with a number of famous local scholars or ulema. At his first stop in Siirt, Nursi was challenged by the local ulema for the first time and was successful in debating with them and answering their questions. He moved on to the *medrese* of the famous Molla Fethullah Efendi, who examined Nursi on the texts he had read and learnt. Again, he was able to answer all of the questions with comparative ease. It was from this point onwards that he became known as 'Said-i Meşhur' – the 'famous Said'.

As Nursi's fame was growing, so were his difficulties. He set off for Bitlis again and remained there a while in the *medrese* of Shaykh Emin. It was there that he was to encounter a certain hostility on the part of local scholars, jealous of Nursi's burgeoning popularity and reputation. It is reported that Shaykh Emin subjected him to another examination, which he passed successfully. He then went to the Kureyş mosque, where he began to preach. This opportunity provided him with a new set of followers and increased his popularity even more. As a consequence, two factions formed in the town: one supporting Nursi and the other supporting Shaykh Emin. In the end, pressures exerted on him by the local authorities led to his decision to leave. He made his way to Tillo, from where he continued to Cizre and then on to Mardin.

At this point, it is important to see the Eastern provinces of the late Ottoman Empire in their historical context.[1] In the words of the missionary, Isabella Bird Bishop, who visited the area in 1891: 'Bitlis is one of the roughest and most fanatical and turbulent of Turkish cities, but the present governor, Rauf Pasha, is a man of energy and has reduced the town and neighbourhood to some degree of order' (cited in Mardin, 'Shaping of a Vocation', 72).

According to Bruinessen's *Agha, Shaikh and State* (50–122), the Eastern provinces in the late Ottoman period were under the political and/or economic control of tribally organized Kurds, so that tribal structure was superimposed upon quasi-feudal power relations. In the nineteenth century, chieftains of big tribes competed for adherents among the tribesmen and for power derived from the Ottoman state. The one exception to this was action led by shaykhs, the only authorities to enjoy the loyalty of sections of more than one tribe. The shaykhs in the region derived their political and economic leverage from association with the Divine. Through the Sufi Orders they were in contact with other parts of the

---

1 For a concise account of that context, see Mardin, 'Shaping of a Vocation', 73–7.

region and so potentially capable of mobilizing large masses. While many dervish orders existed in the Muslim world, in eastern Anatolia during the late Ottoman era only two were present: the Qadiri and the Naqshbandi. Bruinessen provides some insights into the socio-political changes in the region and some clues as to why many people turned to religion and to the shaykhs primarily – to find the security and assurance lacking in their lives. He also outlines the characteristics of the Naqshbandi order and explains why it spread so rapidly in the region.

In Mardin, Molla Said was first 'awakened politically' when he became aware of the wider issues facing the Muslim world through meetings with certain travellers who were passing through the town. The first of these was a follower of Jamal al-Din al-Afghani, one of the prominent architects of the pre-modern reformist tradition; the second was a member of the Sanusi Order, which had provided a religious framework for the formation of a modern nation state in North Africa.

Unhappy with Nursi's activities in Mardin, in 1892 the governor sent Nursi under guard to Bitlis. There, Nursi's abilities and his characteristically fearless defence of what he believed was right so impressed the governor, Ömer Pasha, that the latter invited him to move into his residence in order to teach his children. During his two-year stay, Nursi had the opportunity to study all of the important classical texts and to improve his knowledge of the Islamic sciences. He also began a study of the natural sciences. From Bitlis, Nursi moved to Van, where, at the initial invitation of the governor, Hasan Pasha, he was to stay for the next fifteen years. After the appointment of Hasan Pasha's successor, Tahir Pasha, Nursi accepted the request to move into the governor's residence. Tahir Pasha was a respected official of the sultan Abdülhamid II. A renowned patron of learning, he owned an extensive library and followed developments in modern science and technology with great enthusiasm. Tahir Pasha was the first state official to recognize Nursi's considerable talent and potential, and continued to give him encouragement and support until his death in 1913.

While in Van, Molla Said continued to study the Islamic sciences in depth. It is said that during this period he was able to memorize approximately ninety important classical texts, all of which he treated as steps to ascend to the truths of the Qur'an directly. It was at this point that he felt able to declare: 'I do not need anything else: the Qur'an alone is sufficient for me' (Şahiner, *Kronolojik Hayatı*, 81). He also took the opportunity to read the newspapers and journals supplied to the governor's office and to use Tahir Pasha's library. He was able to gain knowledge thereby of the broader problems facing Ottoman society and the wider Muslim world. It was probably at this juncture that he realized for the first time that traditional Muslim theology alone was unable to answer the doubts concerning Islam that had been raised as a result of the growth of materialism, and that a study of modern science was necessary. Taking advantage of the facilities at his disposal, he set about studying a whole range of social and natural sciences, including history, geography, mathematics, geology, physics, chemistry, astronomy, and philosophy.

Nursi's official biography states that it was during these years that the ulema gave him the title 'Bediüzzaman' ('nonpareil of the times' or 'wonder of the age'), owed chiefly to the speed and facility with which he comprehended the new secular sciences. Having believed in the necessity of the establishment of a new pedagogy, he developed his ideas on educational reform and created his own particular method of teaching, combining the religious sciences with modern sciences in the belief that the latter would corroborate and strengthen the truths of religion. This objective was of the utmost importance to Nursi throughout his life.

1899–1918

One of the trusted advisers of the Ottoman palace, Yahya Nüzhet Pasha, must have noticed Molla Said's activities and popularity in eastern Anatolia, for after meeting with him in Erzincan, he suggested that Nursi act as adviser to a select committee at the court of Sultan Abdülhamid II. Yahya Nüzhet Pasha wrote a letter of recommendation to the Sultan's Imperial 'Birdkeeper', Kuşçubaşı Mustafa Bey, and gave it to Nursi to deliver personally.[2] Nursi had his own reasons for wanting to move to the capital city of the Ottoman Empire. He was of the opinion that establishing a university in eastern Anatolia, where his new method of teaching would be practised, and where modern science would be taught side by side with the religious disciplines, was essential if the ignorance, backwardness and socio-political problems of the Eastern provinces were to be addressed. Although Nursi was not successful in attracting support for his project on this occasion, he nevertheless struck up a friendship with Mustafa Bey's son, Eşref Sencer Kuşçubaşı, who was later to become a leading figure in the secret service (Teşkilat-ı Mahsusa) of the Young Turks. After spending a year and a half in Istanbul, Said Nursi set off for Van once more, teaching in the

---

[2] Mardin, *Religion and Social Change*, 78. Elsewhere ('Shaping of a Vocation', 71) Mardin writes: 'Nursi must have convinced either his audience of bureaucrats or his followers that he did, indeed, have something to contribute to the defence of Islam because shortly thereafter (1896) he was taken in tow by one of Sultan Abdülhamid's advisors, Yahya Nüzhet Paşa, who was in Iraq in an administrative capacity.'

Horhor *medrese* and studying newspaper articles about Islam and the Muslim world. He returned to Istanbul in 1907.

According to one source (Vahide, *Intellectual Biography*, 33), Nursi's intention in returning to the Ottoman capital was to try to gain official support for his idea of an Islamic university, the Medresetü'z-Zehra in eastern Anatolia. Şerif Mardin, however, suggests that it was Nursi's desire to present a series of reform proposals to the Sultan which prompted him to move to Istanbul (*Religion and Social Change*, 79). Nursi settled in the Şekerci *han*, which, according to Mardin, was the centre of Muslim intelligentsia such as Mehmed Akif, the poet who penned the words of the Turkish National Anthem and one of the theoreticians of Muslim revivalism. It was at this *han* that Nursi was to hang an attractive sign on the door of his room, declaring that 'Here, all questions are answered and all problems are solved, but no questions are asked' (Şahiner, *Kronolojik Hayatı*, 91). As expected, many scholars and laymen visited him to ask questions which they had prepared. The debates which grew out of these visits increased his fame and reputation among religious and political leaders, several of whom even 'sought his assistance in connection with questions asked of them by the Commander-in-Chief of the Japanese Army' (Vahide, 'Life and Times of Nursi', 214).

Nursi's stay in Istanbul afforded him his greatest opportunity to publicize the social and educational problems of the Eastern provinces. And on this occasion he succeeded in presenting a report on his ideas concerning reform to the Sultan. Nursi wrote:

> The religious sciences are the light of the conscience, and the modern sciences are the light of reason. The truth becomes manifest through the combining of the two. The students' endeavour will take flight on these two wings. When they are separated it gives rise to bigotry in the one, and wiles and scepticism in the other. (Nursi, *Risale-i Nur Kulliyatı*, 1956)

Towards the end of the Ottoman Empire, Istanbul and the Sultanate were home to numerous political intrigues. Consequently, as Nursi became respected by the ulema of Istanbul and gained a large popular following, there were rivals, jealous of his success. So when, in a meeting with Sultan Abdülhamid, the bold language Nursi used in the petition he proposed was deemed offensive, he was arrested and later sent to the Topkapı mental asylum. Declared sane, he was then offered compensation and a monthly salary. He rejected both, saying 'I am not here to beg for a salary; I would not accept it even if it were a thousand liras. I have not come here for personal gain; I have come here for my nation. Furthermore, this bribe that you want to give me is nothing but hush-money' (Şahiner, *Kronolojik Hayatı*, 103).

Later we find Said Nursi in Salonica, where he stayed as a guest in the house of Manyasızade Refik Bey, chairman of the Committee of Union and Progress (CUP) and later Minister of Justice in the first Cabinet following the proclamation of the Constitution. Three days after the Young Turks' military coup against Abdülhamid, Nursi delivered a speech titled 'Address to Freedom' in Istanbul, repeating it later in Salonica's Freedom Square. The speech was organized by the CUP, but although Nursi was one of its supporters, he nevertheless criticized the deleterious social consequences of their misrule.

Nursi actually considered support for constitutionalism to be a religious obligation. For, he argued, as long as it was consonant with the corpus of Islamic injunctions, it would be 'the means of upholding the might of Islam and exalting the word of God' (Vahide, 'Life and Times', 216). In his view, upholding the word of God (*ila-yı kelimetullah*) is contingent in part on material progress, and since constitutionalism was one way to achieve progress, it was incumbent on all to work for it.

From this point onwards, Nursi became very involved in political and social life. Between the years 1908 and 1910, he made use of the new freedoms of thought and expression to deliver speeches, address gatherings and publish numerous articles in the newspapers and journals of the day. He was also a member of a number of societies, including the Talebe-i Ulum Cemiyeti (Society for Students of the Sciences) and the İttihad-ı Muhammedî Cemiyeti (Society for Muhammadan Unity). It was the latter organization which was accused of inciting the '31st of March Incident'. Said Nursi had been present at its opening ceremony, where he delivered a speech; subsequently he became active in the society, publishing articles in its famous newspaper, *Volkan*. After the 31 March revolt, Nursi was arrested and put on trial by the Military Court. The leading members of the society were tried and hanged. Said Nursi also expected to be hanged, but after his long defence speech (later published), he was acquitted. After the trial, Nursi did not stay long in Istanbul and set off for Van.

During the next two years, Nursi travelled throughout the Eastern provinces, addressing gatherings in which he explained the principles underlying the freedom movement and constitutionalism, maintaining all the time that these principles were not contrary to Islamic injunctions. He invited questions, which he then answered, collating these debates into two volumes: *Münazarat* (The Debates); and *Muhakemat* (The Reasonings), published in 1913 and 1911 respectively. Early in 1911, Nursi visited Damascus, where, at the insistence of the ulema of the city, he preached his famous *Damascus Sermon* in the Umayyad Mosque. Ten thousand people were reported to have attended, including a hundred religious scholars. *The Damascus Sermon* was printed twice in Damascus during the following week. Comprising 'six words' taken from 'the pharmacy of the Qur'an', the sermon prescribes remedies for 'six dire sicknesses'. According to Nursi, these are:

> Firstly, the coming to life and rise of despair and hopelessness in social life. Secondly, the death of truthfulness in social and political life. Thirdly, love of enmity. Fourthly, not knowing the luminous bonds that bind the believers to one another. Fifthly, despotism, which spreads like various contagious diseases. And sixthly, restricting endeavour to what is personally beneficial. (Nursi, *The Damascus Sermon*, 26–7)

The 'treatments' prescribed by Nursi for these ailments were the fostering of hope and true Islamic morality.

Following his stay in Damascus, Said Nursi set off for Istanbul once more to pursue his dream of founding the Medresetü'z-Zehra in eastern Anatolia. This time he almost succeeded. When Sultan Mehmed Reşad set out on his famous journey to Rumeli, Nursi was invited along as representative of the Eastern provinces of the Ottoman Empire. During this journey he was granted nineteen thousand gold liras to establish the university. On his return to Van, he personally selected a site for the university but soon afterwards, the outbreak of the Balkan War meant that the project had to be abandoned.

Before being sent to Tripoli by the Young Turks to encourage the Sanusi resistance against the Italian occupiers, Nursi appears as a very active member in the Young Turks' secret service. This was founded in 1897 in Makka to foster Islamic unity and to support the policy of pan-Islamism; the head of the service was one of Nursi's old friends, Eşref Sencer Kuşçubaşı. Nursi worked for the secret service until 1922, when he went to Ankara, accompanying a group of twenty members. Nursi was one of five who signed a fatwa endorsing jihad, calling on all Muslims to join the war in support of the Caliph against the Central Powers in the First World War (Mermer, *Aspects of Religious Identity*, 503).

Enver Pasha, Minister of War between 1914–1918, wanted Nursi to mobilize a militia composed of four to five thousand men on the Caucasian front. Nursi made his own students the centre of this force, which he commandeered on the Caucasian front in 1916. During the war he began a Qur'anic commentary entitled *İşârâtü'l-İ'câz* (Signs of Miraculousness), despite the unfavourable physical conditions at the front.

Nursi was wounded in battle and, after the fall of Bitlis, was captured and sent to a prisoner of war camp in Kostroma. After two years in captivity, Nursi was able to take advantage of the chaos caused by the Communist Revolution and managed to escape, returning to Istanbul via Petersburg, Warsaw, Berlin and Vienna. Shortly after his arrival, he was awarded a medal for his war service.

Looking back over the first period of Nursi's life, we can see important internal and external factors that had a bearing on his personality. Said Nursi was born in the dying years of the Ottoman Empire. The Caliphate had become the main target of foreign forces, and the collapse of the 'sick man of Europe' was imminent. This was the political atmosphere in which Said Nursi grew up.

Nursi received his early education from various *medreses* in the Eastern provinces, some of them associated with the Naqshbandi Order. At the age of eight or nine, despite the fact that all of Nursi's relatives were members of that Order, Nursi started to take sides against them in favour of 'Abd al Qadir al-Jilani and Ahmad Sirhindi (Imam Rabbani), whom Nursi called 'the Highest Saints'. As Mardin points out, this detail might have been added to his biography later by Nursi himself. Şerif Mardin argues that its function would have been to underpin the idea that Said Nursi had brought many new elements to Khalidi teachings and therefore deserved to be seen as the founder of a new branch. Such a claim to originality is, according to Mardin, supported by Nursi's tendency to cite Sirhindi more often than Mevlana Khalid.

Nevertheless, as will be argued in later chapters, Nursi always pointed out that he understood Sufism to be inappropriate for the modern age. A conversation between Nursi and Shaykh Mehmed Jalali of the Doğubayazit Medrese mentioned earlier in this chapter supports Nursi's views in this regard. During this conversation, Nursi gives a clue to the reasons for his inability to settle in any *medrese*. According to Mardin, this inability betokened the remarkably modern perception of a peasant boy, born in a village of twenty houses, of the insufficiency of the existing education system. Mardin concludes:

> Gradually, then, Said was moving towards a rejection of the *şeyhly* social structure into which he was born and was gathering strength from sources which were part of that world but which hovered above the existing set of social relations controlled by *şeyhs*.[3]

This was the period in which he started his 'first political life'. The expression possibly denotes a widening of his intellectual horizons, which resulted from meetings with students of theology who were passing through the town of Mardin.

During this first period of his life, Said Nursi 'began to sense the growing need for a fresh exposition and defence of the Qur'anic message in the face of modern materialism' (Mermer, *Aspects of Religious Identity*, 486). It is probably after these educational experiences that Nursi realized the need for a new Qur'anic commentary – one which, he believed, would prove the truths of belief by a new method which

[3] Mardin, *Religion and Social Change*, 69. Elsewhere ('Shaping of a Vocation', 67), Mardin writes: 'He did not spare his criticism for the leading figures among the şeyhs of Bitlis whom he accused of fleecing the poor and later, in the 1920s, he stated that he understood how one could criticize the "bourgeoisie" for its egotism.'

blended science with the truths of religion, and which would address the mentality of modern man and confront the dangers of materialist philosophy.

It was also in this period, at the birth of the twentieth century, that Nursi gradually made the transition from teaching to writing.

THE PERIOD OF TRANSITION: 1918–1925

After arriving in Istanbul, Said Nursi was immediately granted membership of the Dârü'l-Hikmeti'l-İslâmiye (The Academy of Higher Islamic Studies) as a nominee of the army. The Dârü'l-Hikmeti'l-İslâmiye was a learned institution founded to find solutions to the problems facing the Muslim world and to respond to attacks upon it; to disseminate publications informing the people of Turkey of their religious duties; and to uphold Islamic morality. Branches were opened in all provinces and major towns. Members included Mehmed Akif, its first Secretary (Başkatip); İzmirli İsmail Hakkı; Elmalılı Hamdi Yazır; Mustafa Sabri Efendi; and Saadettin Pasha. All of them prominent religious scholars, the members were divided into three committees: jurisprudence (*fiqh*), ethics (*akhlāq*) and theology (*kalām*). It was also at this time that, with the support of Enver Pasha, the Minister of War, Nursi's partial Qur'anic commentary, 'The Signs of Miraculousness', was published.

In 1920, at the recommendation of the *shaykh al-islām*, Musâ Kazım Bey, Nursi was appointed to the rank of *mahreç* (*şehü'l-islam*) by Sultan Vahdettin. Over the next few years he continued to write and publish on the causes of Ottoman decline: *Sünuhat* (1920), *Hakikat Çekirdekleri* (1920), *Nokta* (1921), *Rumûz* (1922) and *İşârât* (1923) were all written in this period.

Nursi also promoted the foundation of organizations and societies such as the Yeşilay (Green Crescent Society) in 1920, and the Cemiyet-i Müderrisin (The Medrese Teachers' Association), founded in January 1921. He was also invited to take part in the establishment of a Kurdish state. Nursi was dismissive, replying allegedly that '...rather than establish a Kurdish state, it is necessary to revive the Ottoman empire'.[4]

When the *shaykh al-islām*, Dürrizade Abdullah Efendi, issued a fatwa to outlaw the national independence groups, Nursi issued a counter-fatwa justifying the existence of such groups and declaring the national struggle a jihad. According to Mardin (*Religion and Social Change*, 94), 'the Ankara government formed in opposition to that of the Sultan seems to have been impressed, and invited him to join the movement.' Nursi joined the independence groups a week before the *'Īd al-aḍḥa* (the Feast of the Sacrifices 'Kurban Bayramı') and, at the invitation of Mustafa Kemal, President of the Grand National Assembly, was invited to Ankara. He arrived there on 4 August 1922 to a huge welcome.

Following the victory of the National Army in the War of Independence, Nursi was given an official welcome in the Grand National Assembly on 9 November 1922. However, he was sorely disappointed with the situation in Ankara. Before leaving Istanbul, Said Nursi had been of the opinion that it was

> the beginning of a new era and exactly the time to marshal their forces to make the new Republic the means for bringing about a renaissance

---

4 Şahiner, *Kronolojik Hayatı*, 228. From this point on Nursi was always targeted as a Kurdish nationalist, often being mistaken for the Naqshbandi leader, Shaykh Said, who led a revolt with the explicit aim of establishing an independent Kurdish state. See Bruinessen, *Agha, Shaikh and State*, 65, 81, 258.

> of Islam and Islamic civilisation, and make it a centre and source of support for the Islamic world. (Vahide, *Intellectual Biography*, 178; see also: Nursi, *Risale-i Nur Kulliyatı*, 2138.)

However, once in Ankara, Nursi realized much to his chagrin that the government was pursuing the politics of secularization. Atheistic ideas of philosophic materialism were being propagated, and deputies were demonstrating a lax attitude towards Islam and their religious obligations. Consequently, Nursi saw fit to issue a declaration demanding that they adhere to Islam and fulfil their religious duties; it is said that as a result of his entreaty, fifty to sixty deputies began to perform their daily prayers regularly.

Despite this small measure of success, Nursi decided eventually that he must leave Ankara. Mustafa Kemal had asked him either to be a deputy for Muş or to perform a role similar to that undertaken by Shaykh Sanusi in Libya; Nursi declined on both counts. According to Abu-Rabi (ed. *Islam at the Crossroads*, 64), the meeting Nursi had with Kemal Atatürk was, following his transformation into the 'New Said' several years before, the most momentous event in his life. He (Nursi) predicted that Turkey that was at the crossroads, his ideas on the role of religion in the new Turkey being almost diametrically opposed to those of Mustafa Kemal and his supporters. Yet Nursi's experience in Ankara was not entirely negative, for he was able during his stay to publish two important works: *Zeylü'l-Zeyl* and *Hubab*, both of which had the objective of combating atheism. He also obtained 150,000 liras for the establishment of his Eastern University.

Said Nursi moved back to Van, where he was to stay for nearly two years. In the summer months, he lived on the slopes of Mount Erek, where he devoted himself entirely to contemplation rather than writing or teaching; in the winter, he took up residence in the Nurşin Mosque, situated in the Toprakkale district of the town. Again, Nursi was successful in attracting many students, and the attention of large numbers of religious scholars and shaykhs. He preached at the mosque every Friday, but on the fundamentals of belief rather than on political and social events and developments. This signifies a new direction for him, given the fact that up until now he had been seeking to revive Islam and society by means of politics.

In February 1925, some time after the abolition of the Caliphate, the so-called 'Shaykh Said Revolt' broke out. Shaykh Said of Palu, the Naqshbandi leader, had requested Nursi to join his side in the revolt, but Nursi declined, replying in writing:

> The Turkish nation has acted as the standard-bearer of Islam for centuries. It has produced many saints and given many martyrs. The sword may not be drawn against the sons of such a nation. We are Muslims, we are their brothers, and we may not make brother fight brother. It is not permissible according to the Shariʿa. The sword is to be drawn against external enemies, it may not be used internally. Our only salvation at this time is to offer illumination and guidance through the truths of the Qur'an and belief; it is to get rid of our greatest enemy, ignorance. Give up this attempt of yours, for it will be fruitless. Thousands of innocent men and women may perish on account of a few bandits. (Vahide, *Intellectual Biography*, 191–3)

The Revolt was quashed within two months, culminating in exile, imprisonment and execution for those involved.

Although Nursi's warnings with regard to the Revolt saved many lives in the Van area, he himself was later accused of having links to the rebels. After being questioned in Istanbul about his part in the affair, Nursi was taken to Antalya by boat and from there to Burdur, a small town in southwestern Anatolia, where he was to stay for the next seven months. His arrival in Burdur marked the beginning of a number of periods of exile and house arrest for Nursi, authorized by the government. During his stay in Burdur, he settled in the Haji Abdullah Mosque in the Değirmenler district of the town, where he taught, wrote and, inevitably, attracted the attention of the local people. Everyday after afternoon prayers he would preach, later collecting these *dersler* ('sermons' or 'teachings') into a book entitled *Nur'un İlk Kapısı* (The First Door of the *Risale-i Nur*). According to Vahide (*Intellectual Biography*, 197), these were the first fruits of Nursi's period of deep reflection and contemplation in Van which were later to find full expression in the *Risale-i Nur*; they also represented the first instructions the New Said claimed to have received directly from the Qur'an.

However, Nursi's increasing popularity perturbed the authorities and eventually led them in 1926 to take him to Isparta, in south-western Anatolia. There he stayed for three weeks in the *medrese* of Müftü Tahsin Efendi, but before long his teaching and concomitant popularity came to the attention of the authorities, who decided this time to send him away to a small, remote place where he would not attract followers and where, deprived of all company and society, he would just fade away and be forgotten. The place they chose was the village of Barla, a tiny hamlet of 15 to 20 houses in the mountains near the north-western shore of Lake Eğridir.

Although it is beyond the scope of this study to describe in any depth the course of political events during this period, a brief overview will nevertheless be helpful if we are to comprehend the background to Nursi's inner crises.

This period of Nursi's life began shortly after the First World War, the most devastating war in human history, and at the demise of the Ottoman Empire. In Nursi's native country, the successors of that empire founded a republic based on the principles of secularism and Westernization. The Sultanate and the Caliphate were also abolished at this time.

According to his nephew who acted as his secretary during the time, after escaping from the POW camp, Nursi was an active member of Dârü'l-Hikmeti'l-İslâmiye. However, Nursi had been severely shaken by the war, and attempted on several occasions to discontinue his membership. Nevertheless, his sense of duty prevailed and, as he himself put it, the responsibility he felt towards 'the nation' meant that he would continue to serve to the best of his abilities.

Tellingly, Nursi never talked in detail about the two and half years he spent as a prisoner of war in Kostroma or about the manner of his escape and return to Istanbul; nor did he permit his nephew to write about it. According to Vahide (*Intellectual Biography*, viii), this was on account of Nursi's desire to accentuate only those facets of his experience which looked to the 'the fruit' of his life, namely the *Risale-i Nur* and its service to belief and the Qur'an. Nevertheless it is worth noting that one of the reasons for his crisis of conscience was that Nursi had confronted the ideological background of historical materialism either as a prisoner in Kostroma or during the months he was in Germany and Austria on his way back to Istanbul. In many of his later works we read that he identified historical materialism as the *dajjāl* (Antichrist) of the times. Another factor he hints at in one of his later works is the pessimism he saw at the heart of philosophy; this is to be contrasted with the earlier period of his life, in which he had accorded equal importance to the philosophical sciences and religion. Vahide provides us with some insight into Nursi's thought system and the later stages of his life:

> Thus we can say that Bediüzzaman's enlightenment occurred in three stages. Firstly, he realised the deficiency of the 'human philosophy' he had studied and how it had been an obstacle to his enlightenment and progress. And secondly, as Bediüzzaman himself confessed, through the 'bitter medicine' of Shaykh 'Abd al-Qadir Geylani's *Fütûhu'l-Gayb*:

'I understood my faults, perceived my wounds, and my pride was to a degree destroyed.' Then to complete the process of his transformation into the New Said, he understood through the *Mektûbat* of Imam-i Rabbani that he should take the Qur'an as his sole master. The instruction in Divine Unity he then received from the Qur'an through the phrase 'There is no god but God' was 'a most brilliant light' scattering the darkness in which he had been plunged and allowing him to breathe easily. (Vahide, *Intellectual Biography*, 167)

Throughout this period, an active member of Dârü'l-Hikmeti'l-İslâmiye yet affected by a deep spiritual crisis, he regularly withdrew from social life, seeking solitude in places far removed from Istanbul life, such as Yuşa Tepesi, a high hill on the Asian side of the Bosphorus. Also around this time, another event that affected him deeply was his being abandoned by his nephew, a man who was, in Nursi's own words, 'his student, his servant, his secretary, his adopted child' (*Risale-i Nur Kulliyatı*, 710).

And finally, arguably the most important factor which affected Nursi in this period was neglect and abandonment of their religious obligations by officials of the government – a dereliction of duty he attributed to the inadequacy of the education system and the doubts caused by materialist philosophy concerning Islam in this age.

Yet Nursi's inner struggles were to result in the crystallization of his ideas and a spiritual rebirth as he transformed from the 'Old Said' to the 'New Said'.

THE NEW SAID (1926–1948)

Nursi's exile in Barla lasted almost eight and a half years, during which he wrote most of the one hundred and thirty parts of his *Risale-i Nur*. According to Vahide, the main aim of the authorities was to keep him in a remote and isolated place such as Barla in order to obviate as far as possible any kind of contact with the outside world. To this end they had him watched and followed, and attempted to prevent local people approaching him by spreading rumours about him. Although after a time the Government granted an amnesty to those exiled with Nursi, he himself was denied this.

Throughout his eight and a half year stay in Barla, Nursi dedicated himself to the writing of the *Risale-i Nur* and by the end had dictated three quarters, a total of 119 pieces. The first section of the *Risale* written in Barla was a treatise proving the resurrection of the dead and the existence of the hereafter. After that, the *Miraculousness of the Qur'an* was written and by 1929 the first collation of treatises was finished, titled *Sözler* (The Words). *Mektubat* (The Letters), the second main book of the *Risale*, was also completed during this period. As Vahide puts it (*Intellectual Biography*, 204): 'Thus began Bediüzzaman's silent struggle against the forces of irreligion.'

The method of disseminating the *Risale* was as follows: after having written out and distributed the original copies by hand, these were then copied again and passed on to others, who would write out further copies. In this way *The Words* passed from village to village, and in the course of time, from town to town, and on throughout Turkey. According to some sources, the number of hand-written copies of the various parts of the *Risale-i Nur* totals some sixty thousand. Others consider this figure to be obviously exaggerated, but it is an indication that Nursi's message was spreading around the country, and with it his following.

Besides the main components of the *Risale-i Nur*, the supplementary letters Nursi wrote to his students, together with some of their replies, were compiled in three volumes under the title *Lâhikalar* (The Appendices). In later years they were included in the *Risale-i Nur*; one of the most well-known was entitled *Barla Lâhikası* (The Barla Appendix).

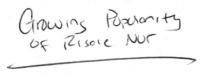

The growing popularity of *Risale-i Nur* and the increase in Nursi's followers forced the authorities to redouble their efforts to exert pressure on Nursi and the students of the *Risale*, especially after a new law was passed prohibiting the reciting in Arabic of the call to prayer. At the end of summer of 1934, Nursi was taken from Barla back to Isparta, where he spent the next nine months. Yet he continued to write while he was there, finishing *Lem'alar* (The Flashes), the third book of the *Risale*, while in Eskişehir prison.

On 25 April 1935, 120 of his students from all over Turkey, including Van, were arrested and held in custody. Two days later, Nursi himself was arrested. The officials were alarmed by reports in the press of a 'countrywide network of reactionaries'. Rumour had it that Nursi and his followers were to be executed. They were accused, amongst other things, of having founded 'an illegal secret society, aimed at undermining the present regime and destroying the fundamental principles of the state'. The Home Affairs Minister, Shükrü Kaya, and the Commander-in-Chief of the Gendarmerie moved to Isparta from Ankara at the head of a detachment of gendarmes. Control of Isparta was guaranteed by the military units, and cavalry were positioned along the road all the way from Isparta to Afyon. The accused were taken in lorries to Eskişehir prison, where they were to remain for the duration of the trial. There, as well as completing *Lem'alar* (The Flashes), Nursi would begin to write *Şualar* (The Rays), the fourth book of the *Risale-i Nur*. Nursi was later to refer to the prison as the Medrese-i Yusufiye (the School of Joseph), recalling the incarceration of the Prophet Joseph, the patron-saint of prisoners.

Nursi was sentenced to eleven months imprisonment for writing a short treatise expounding some Qur'anic verses about Islamic dress. Fifteen of his students were sentenced to six months and the remaining 105 acquitted. Nursi objected to the verdict, arguing that a sentence like this should be given only to a horse thief or a kidnapper; he demanded to be given his freedom or, if truly guilty of any crime, to be sentenced to execution or one hundred and one years of imprisonment. Nursi was released from Eskişehir prison in the spring of 1936 and sent once more into exile, this time to Kastamonu in the the Black Sea region of Anatolia. There, Nursi's first place of residence was the local police station, where he stayed as a 'guest' for three months. Afterwards he moved to rented accommodation opposite the police station, where he would live for the next seven years.

Before long, Nursi began again to attract new students, while maintaining correspondence with followers in other parts of the country, particularly in Isparta. The letters he wrote to his students can be found in his *Kastamonu Lâhikası* (The Kastamonu Appendix) in the *Risale-i Nur.*

It was also in Kastamonu that he wrote one of the most important treatises that make up the *Risale-i Nur*, his magisterial *Âyetü'l-Kübra* (The Supreme Sign). Nursi also completed some sections of *Şualar* (The Rays) collection, one of which – the 'Fifth Ray' – concerned Prophetic traditions on signs of the end of time. According to Vahide:

> The final draft of this treatise had been made in 1938 from a first draft made while Bediüzzaman was a member of the Darü'l-Hikmet from pieces some of which were taken from *Muhâkemat*, published in 1909. (Vahide, *Intellectual Biography*, 269–70)

On 31 August 1943, ostensibly on account of his writing and dissemination of the treatise on the 'end times', Nursi and twenty-two of his students were arrested and held in custody at Kastamonu police station. The trial took place in Denizli, where a total of 126 students – those originally detained in Kastamonu and a large number arrested in Isparta and elsewhere – were imprisoned:

As with the Eskishehir affair, the matter was taken up by Ankara and blown up out of all proportion. President İsmet İnönü, Prime Minister Şükrü Saraçoğlu, and Education Minister Hasan Ali Yücel were directly concerned. Instructions were sent to Isparta and ü in particular, and the houses of numerous *Risale-i Nur* students searched. Then the arrests started in Isparta. (Vahide, *Intellectual Biography*, 271)

The criminal court appointed a committee of experts to deal with the case. Nursi objected immediately, pointing out that that the committee was composed of local officials rather than religious experts:

A high committee of well-educated experts should examine the *Risale-i Nur* in Ankara. Philosophers should be brought from Europe (to participate in the committee). If they find any offence against the law [in the *Risale-i Nur*] I will not object to the heaviest penalty.
(Nursi, *Risale-i Nur Kulliyatı*, 2182)

Nursi stood accused of creating a new Sufi *tarikat*; forming a political society; opposing the reforms; and exploiting religious feelings, particularly with his treatise concerning the end of time. The committee of experts was made up of Professor Yusuf Ziya Yörükan of the Advisory Board for the President of Religious Affairs, Necati Lugal from the Middle East Institute of the Faculty of Language, History and Geography, and Yusuf Aykut, a member of the Council for Collection of Islamic Books in the Turkish Historical Society. Their report was unexpectedly favourable, confirming that nine-tenths of the *Risale-i Nur* comprised scholarly explanations of the truths of belief, and that since these were of a purely religious nature, there was no need for them to be proscribed. The Court subsequently cleared all of Nursi's works, acquitted all the prisoners, including Nursi himself, and ruled that they be released immediately. This decision came on 16 July 1944 after nine months of imprisonment, during which two of Nursi's students had died. According to Vahide

(*Intellectual Biography*, 277), the imprisonment and trials actually served Nursi's goals, since the publicity generated by the court case focused attention on Nursi and his students more acutely than ever before. That the trial ended with a clean bill of health for Nursi's teachings meant that the *Risale-i Nur* would attract even more readers, including those who moved in official circles.

As usual, during his imprisonment Nursi continued to write, but this time in secrecy and with the greatest of difficulty, given that paper was denied him. Consequently, it was alleged that materials such as matchboxes were used for writing, although this may be something of an exaggeration. Later, restrictions were eased by prison officials when they realized the beneficial effect that Nursi's writings were having on the inmates, and so Nursi's followers were allowed to copy and distribute the writings among their fellow prisoners. Among these writings, the *Fruits of Belief*, the *Eleventh Ray* and defence speeches of Nursi and his students were added to the *Risale-i Nur*.

After a stay of nearly two months in the Şehir Hotel in Denizli, Nursi was taken on government instructions to Emirdağ, a small provincial town situated between Afyon and Eskişehir, from where he was forbidden to move. Nursi stayed in Emirdağ for the next seven years, with a break of twenty months in Afyon prison between January 1948 and October 1949.

It is arguably on account of the favourable outcome of the Denizli trials that Nursi and the *Risale* now began to acquire unprecedented fame throughout Turkey. Up to this point, Nurcu activity had been concentrated mainly in two or three areas; following the trial, many thousands of people across the country became students of Nursi's teachings and began to serve both the *Risale* and the cause of the Qur'an in various ways. Furthermore, around this time, two of the first duplicating machines to appear in Turkey were purchased by Nursi's students: one was set up in Isparta and the other in İnebolu, and copies of the *Risale-i Nur* now became available on a far wider scale.

Nursi continued to pursue his writing and attract an increasing number of students. The 'Tenth Matter' of the *Fruits of Belief*, the first nine of which had been written in Denizli prison, was written at this time, along with a reply to objections raised about repetition in the Qur'an and a treatise on the nature and function of angels. With these treatises, the *Risale-i Nur* was gradually approaching completion. Nursi also produced *Asâ-yı Mûsa* (The Staff of Moses) and *Zülfikar*, collations of sections and passages taken from the main components of the *Risale*, namely *The Words*, *The Letters*, *The Flashes* and *The Rays*, with the aim of combating atheism and unbelief. With the same goal, *A Guide for Youth* was printed in 1947 in Eskişehir, aimed chiefly at schoolchildren. For the sake of the younger generation who had no knowledge of the Arabic script, these later writings appeared in the newly introduced Latin alphabet. However, most of the collections of the *Risale* continued to be published in the Arabic-Ottoman script.

The *Risale-i Nur* was also beginning to filter through slowly to the rest of the Muslim world. Nursi had copies of both *The Staff of Moses* and *Zülfikar* sent to al-Azhar in Egypt, to Damascus and Madina, and to a number of religious scholars in the Indian subcontinent. Nursi's students also established relations with some American missionaries and gave them copies of the aforementioned works, the aim being to counter the growing threat of communism. In accordance with certain Prophetic Traditions, Nursi believed implicitly in co-operation with Christians against the threat of unbelief. (See Nursi, *Risale-i Nur Külliyatı*, 82 and 1744.)

During his stay in Emirdağ, Nursi spent most of his time correcting both handwritten and duplicated copies of the *Risale*. He also continued to correspond with his students more energetically than before: the letters written by Nursi to encourage his students and direct their activities were later added to the *Risale-i Nur* under the title of *Emirdağ Lâhikası 1* (The Emirdağ Appendix 1).

Nursi's situation, however, was soon to take a turn for the worse when, on 23 January 1948, he and 54 of his students were arrested and detained in Afyon prison. The charges levelled against them were virtually identical to those in the past: they were accused of founding a secret political society; of opposing the present regime; and of trying to destroy the fundamental principles of the state. Nursi was placed in solitary confinement in an unheated cell. According to some sources, Nursi was poisoned a total of seventeen times during his spells in exile and imprisonment, including his incarceration in Afyon. One of his closest students, Mustafa Sungur, recorded Nursi's words:

> Perhaps I will not be able to survive. Let my whole being be sacrificed to the fatherland, the nation, our youth and the rest of the Muslim world, and also for the sake of eternal well being and the felicity of mankind. If I die, let my friends not seek any vengeance for me. (Şahiner, *Kronolojik Hayatı*, 368)

His supporters called Nursi's imprisonment in Afyon the third 'School of Joseph' (*Medrese-i Yusufiye*). They continued copying the *Risale* by hand, while Nursi himself wrote *El-Hüccetü'z-Zehra*, the 15th part of *The Rays* and the final component of the *Risale-i Nur* collection. Scrap paper and paper bags were used as writing materials.

On 6 December 1948, the Afyon criminal court delivered its verdict and sentenced Nursi to twenty months of imprisonment; twenty of his students were sentenced to six months.

The verdict was immediately sent to the Supreme Court, which overturned the lower court's decision and acquitted him. After spending twenty months in custody throughout the duration of the trial, Nursi was finally released on 20 September 1949.

This period – from the adoption of the Swiss Civil Code in the republic of Turkey and the concomitant disestablishment of Islam until the end of the Second World War – was a time when the Muslim world lost its unity and succumbed to the depredations of the colonialist powers. It was a period in which secular and materialistic ideologies were becoming increasingly influential in determining the orientation of political systems, and in which Muslim societies underwent some of the most radical changes they had experienced since the outset of Islamic civilization in the seventh century. As Dursun says

> The period in which the *Risale-i Nur* was written, which constituted Said Nursi's most important activity, was the single party period, during which religion was excised from politics and the social structure, wrenched out of people's hearts, and positivism gradually began to be influential. (Dursun, 'Nursi as Representative of Social Opposition', 317)

Nursi was not wholly unprepared for the radical changes and developments occurring in Turkey. His stay in Ankara had made him realize that any attempt to ameliorate the situation politically would be fruitless, given that the policies of the new Turkish republic were based on secular materialism. He responded to this by emphasizing his belief that the Qur'an was the only truth and reality, and that man's true happiness and progress could be achieved through adoption of new forms of education and theology. Thus in this period he dedicated his life to writing new treatises in which, according to Vahide (*Intellectual Biography*, 226), he dealt with the irrefutable truths of belief and demonstrated the logical absurdity of materialist philosophy, making it possible for man to attain belief so firm and certain that it could withstand any doubts caused by science or philosophy.

Up until the period of the 'New Said', it is clear that Nursi's struggle in the name of Islam was effected chiefly by means of his active involvement in social and political life. From 1926 onwards, however, we no longer see Said Nursi as an activist on the socio-political stage. Instead, Nursi led a solitary life of persecution, and of total opposition to positivism and materialism:

> The distinction Bediüzzaman made between the periods of the Old Said and the New Said reflect the difference between the first and second periods of the Islamic world. Bediüzzaman, who as the Old Said in the first period was actively involved in trying to bring about the political reforms necessary for the Islamic world, in the second period as the New Said, undertook to renew the belief of Muslim individuals, and to form a community or group of these individuals, rather than re-establishing the political structure of the Islamic world, which had entered a period of complete political suspension (*fetret*). (Davutoğlu, 'Bediüzzaman and the Politics of the 20th Century Islamic World', 301)

Nursi's main concern was the strengthening of the individual's belief and the search for solutions to the important questions thrown up by human existence. As he himself averred, serving Islam by means of politics is of little significance when compared with serving it through belief.

Besides his main work, *Risale-i Nur*, there was continual correspondence between Nursi and his students. In his letters, Nursi encouraged his students to continue to write out the *Risale*. He offered them guidance and encouraged unity amongst them, warning them to treat their enemies with caution. He also stressed the necessity of avoiding political involvement of any sort and the need for them to develop complete sincerity in their service to the cause.

According to Vahide (*Intellectual Biography*, 238–9), Nursi was responsible during this period for informing officials about communism, an ideology that had already overrun Russia and Eastern Europe, and threatened to lead to destabilization and anarchy elsewhere. Nursi was also of the opinion that through the establishment of atheistic organizations, the spread of absolute unbelief in Turkey was being planned and enacted.

By the end of this period, as the *Risale-i Nur* spread and became established, Nursi gathered some of its sections into special collections and, in 1942 and 1943, had them typed out in the new Latin alphabet. Nursi was particularly encouraged by the enthusiastic response the *Risale* was receiving from women and young people.

NURSI THE MASTER (1949–1960)

In the early morning of 20 September 1949, after being released from Afyon prison, Nursi was escorted by two police officers to a house which had been rented by some of his students. Nursi stayed there for two months before moving back to his former house in Emirdağ. On his return, one of the first things he did was to write a letter to the Director of Religious Affairs, Ahmed Hamid Akseki, requesting that the latter do everything possible to ensure the publication and free circulation of the *Risale-i Nur*; he also asked him to print the 'miraculous' Qur'an that Nursi's student Hüsrev had written showing the 'coinciding vertical juxtaposition' (*tevafukat*) of the word Allah and other divine names. Although Ahmed Hamdi agreed in principle to publish the *Risale*, the project never came to fruition.

After the victory of the Democrat Party of Adnan Menderes in the general election of May 1950, the Turkish Republic experienced a real multi-party democratic system for the first time since its establishment. Throughout this period, Nursi and his followers found that they had greater freedom in pursuing activities connected with the *Risale* and the growth of the Nur movement in general. As restrictions eased, a new generation of students, based primarily in Istanbul and Ankara, set about printing and publishing the entire *Risale-i Nur* collection on modern printing presses and in the new Latin alphabet. Consequently, the number of readers and students of the *Risale* grew exponentially, reaching many hundreds of thousands within a relatively short space of time. As Nursi himself said frequently: 'From now on there is no need for me to work in the service of the *Risale-i Nur*. That is to say, the *Risale-i Nur* and its students will perform my duties' (*Risale-i Nur Kulliyatı*, 1094).

Following his release from Afyon prison and his return to Emirdağ, some of his students who had known him of old began to note certain changes in his life. Nursi now kept company with his students in the same house, allowing his food to be prepared by them rather than by the Çalışkan family, who had previously seen to his culinary needs. According to Vahide (*Intellectual Biography*, 334), 'in many respects these last ten years of Bediüzzaman's life may be seen as directing and training these young students and preparing some of them to lead the *Risale-i Nur* movement in later years.' Nursi also began to read daily newspapers again, paying attention to social life and developments in Turkey and the wider Muslim world. When the Democrat Party came to power, the ban on the Arabic call to prayer and the restrictions on Nursi's movements were lifted, and he was therefore able to join the congregation in the *Çarşı* Mosque for *teravih* (*tarāwīḥ*) prayers on each of the thirty nights of Ramadan. On the day that the

Democrats won the election, Nursi sent the following telegram to Celâl Bayar, soon to be elected as the new president of the Republic:

> To Celâl Bayar, President of the Republic. We offer our congratulations. May Almighty God grant you every success in the service of Islam, the country and the nation. In the name of the students of the *Risale-i Nur*, of whom I am one, Said Nursi. (*Risale-i Nur Kulliyatı*, 1813; see also Vahide, *Intellectual Biography*, 334)

To this, Nursi received the following reply:

> To Bediüzzaman Said Nursi, Emirdağ. I was exceedingly touched by your cordial congratulations and offer my thanks. Celâl Bayar (*Risale-i Nur Kulliyatı*, 1813)

Despite the general amnesty issued by the Democrat Party and the fact that Nursi and his followers did experience a certain easing up of conditions, they were still subject to pressure from officials, and court actions against them would continue during the 1950s. For example, the public prosecutor initiated a case against him and a young *Risale-i Nur* student, Muhsin Alev, who had published *Gençlik Rehberi* (A Guide for Youth) in Istanbul. The charge was that the book contravened Article 163 of the Penal Code, undermining the principle of secularism and therefore constituting illegal religious propaganda. Nursi's arraignment led to his first visit to Istanbul for twenty-seven years. The event drew huge public attention, on which Vahide comments:

> The three court hearings – and particularly the second and third – attracted literally thousands. Once again the trial served to publicise Bediüzzaman and the *Risale-i Nur* movement in a way those who had instigated it can scarcely have wished. (Vahide, *Intellectual Biography*, 337)

The trial ended in acquittals. Nursi was also acquitted the following year in another court case.

In late 1953, Nursi set off from Istanbul for Isparta, where he wished to spend the remaining years of his life, having expressed a desire to be buried in one of the small villages there. It was at this time that Nursi began to hold readings and formal study sessions (*ders*) for groups of students of the *Risale-i Nur* in Isparta.

In 1956, the court in Afyon issued its final verdict on Nursi's *magnum opus*, declaring that 'there is nothing against the law in the *Risale-i Nur*' (Şahiner, *Kronolojik Hayatı*, 413–14) and subsequently returning all of the seized copies. The *Risale* then began to be printed on modern presses in the new alphabet. Said Nursi had originally wanted the Prime Minister, Adnan Menderes, to have the *Risale* published officially by the state, and although Menderes favoured this, it was not to happen: the only help received from the Prime Minister was the provision of the paper needed for printing. At this point, Dr. Tahsin Tola, a deputy for Isparta, addressed the matter himself, overseeing the printing of *Sözler* (The Words), *Lem'alar* (The Flashes) and *Mektubat* (The Letters). At the same time, students in Istanbul printed ten thousand copies of *The Short Words*, 2500 of which they posted immediately to various places in Anatolia. Also printed were 5000 copies of *A Letter to Women*. Nursi declared: 'Now is the time of the *Risale-i Nur*'s festival. My duty is finished. This is the time I have long waited for. Now I can go' (Şahiner, *Kronolojik Hayatı*, 414–15).

On 12 April 1957, at the invitation of military officers, Nursi attended a ceremony to lay the foundation for the mosque of the 3rd military division in Isparta. In 1958, the authorized biography of Nursi was written and published, selling at a relatively high price for the time.

In late 1959, Nursi embarked on a series of trips to Ankara, Konya and Istanbul. At the age of 83, this showed more than anything Nursi's extraordinary perseverance and self-sacrifice in continuing his struggle against atheism and his service to the cause of belief and the Qur'an. At the invitation of his students from all over Turkey, Nursi visited them and also the *Risale* study centres (*dershane*) that were springing up across the country. During the last few months of his life, Nursi visited Istanbul once, Konya three times, and Ankara four times. On one of his trips to Konya, Nursi expressed a desire to visit the tomb of Mevlana Jalaluddin Rumi. There he found himself surrounded by a large crowd of people and police, even in the precinct of the tomb itself, which the Director of the Museum had opened to the public especially for the sake of Nursi's visit. It is recorded that Nursi said to the police:

> You serve the country's order and security physically, while we serve it in a non-material way. We know you as fellow-officials, so look upon us as fellow-officials too, and not in any other way. For twenty-eight years I have served this country's peace and security, despite imprisonment, exile, and oppression. (Şahiner, *Kronolojik Hayatı*, 421)

Nursi's second visit to Ankara on the 30 December 1959 attracted a huge amount of attention from the media, generating sensational headlines in national newspapers such as Cumhuriyet and Milliyet. According to the reports of his speeches to journalists, Nursi's aim in coming to Ankara was to allay the suspicion of officials and government deputies with regard to the *Risale-i Nur*, particularly since it had been exonerated by numerous court verdicts. Nursi was visited by a huge number of people during his stay in Ankara, including the three deputies of the Democrat Party who had invited him there.

However, on his last attempt to visit Ankara, Nursi was not permitted to enter the city and his car was turned back. According to a radio broadcast, Nursi was to rest in Emirdağ on the advice of the cabinet, and this he did.

After some time in Emirdağ, preparations were made for his return to Isparta. Bidding a sorrowful farewell to the loyal Çalışkan family and all of his students, early on the morning of the 20 March 1960, Nursi and a few of his closest students set off from Isparta to Urfa on what would be his final journey.

Arriving in Urfa the following day, Nursi was settled into the İpek Palas hotel by his students. His arrival led to unrest, with scuffles breaking out between the police and government officials – who, on the orders of the Interior Minister in Ankara, wanted Nursi to return to Isparta – and Nursi's students, the people of Urfa and certain sympathetic officials, who categorically refused to allow the extremely weak and ailing Nursi to be moved.

Despite his obvious frailty, Nursi received all the visitors who came to see him. On his third day in Urfa, at three o'clock in the morning of the 23 March 1960, Said Nursi died in the İpek Palas Hotel in Urfa. Nursi's personal effects amounted to nothing more than a watch, a cloak, a prayer mat, a teapot, glasses, and twenty Turkish liras. Since Said Nursi had never married, his belongings were given to his only surviving brother, Abdülmecid.

Nursi's funeral took place the following day with a huge crowd of people gathered in the Ulu Mosque. The Governor of Urfa, the Mayor, the local garrison commander, the people of Urfa, and those students of the *Risale-i Nur* who had been able to reach Urfa in time for the burial took part in the funeral prayers. Nursi was buried in the Halilürrahman Dergah, where the Prophet Abraham is allegedly buried. During the funeral process, security measures were tightened within and around Urfa by the local gendarmerie and security forces.

On 27 May 1960, two months after Nursi's burial, a military coup occurred. Several weeks later, Nursi's remains were taken from the Halilürrahman Dergah under cover of darkness to an unknown spot in Anatolia on the orders of a so-called 'National Unity Committee'. During the removal of his body, the town was virtually taken over by the army and a strict curfew enforced with no-one allowed out on the streets. Tanks and armoured vehicles were positioned at all key points in the town and the Dergah was surrounded by a tight cordon of soldiers.

The fourth and final period of Nursi's life began shortly after the Second World War and ended at the beginning of the seventh decade of the century. During this time, Turkey was to experience the birth of a multi-party democratic system, after a period in which it had pursued policies of radical Westernization and all but eliminated Islam from the social arena. After the Second World War, the world became bipolar, with the Western bloc led by the USA and the Eastern bloc led by the young Soviet Union. Turkey gravitated with alacrity to the side of the West and adjusted its system of governance to Western standards.[5] In addition, it carried out a series of far-reaching and highly contentious social and political reforms. This period of Nursi's life was also marked by the emergence of numerous Muslim nation-states as the process of decolonization gathered pace. According to Davutoğlu ('Bediüzzaman and the Politics of the 20th Century Islamic World', 288) theoretical debate was focused on the characteristics of these nation-states and the place of Islam within them, and it was against this background that discussion concerning the Islamic State superseded discussion regarding the Caliphate.

These socio-political developments undoubtedly had an effect on Said Nursi's outlook and marked the start of a new

---

5 Dursun, 'Bediüzzaman Said Nursi as the Representative of Social Opposition', 321.

phase of his life, that in which he became the 'Third Said'. As Dursun points out, Nursi appears as a leader of society who was closely concerned with political developments; who informed the government of his appreciation of some of their positive measures; who wrote letters to the government leaders, including the President and the Prime Minister; and who met on numerous occasions with a number of ministers and deputies ('Nursi as Representative of Social Opposition', 321). This is in direct contrast with the preceding period of his life, in which Nursi appeared to be a dissenting voice against most government's policies, asserting that opposition was one's natural right so long as it did not lead to a breakdown of public order and security.

The change during this period in Said Nursi's method of serving the cause of Islam was closely related to tendencies in society in general. Yet, while Nursi did become more involved than before in social and political matters, his support for the Democrats, for example, came in the form of guidance rather than political activism – something which he eschewed throughout the whole of his life. He also forbade his students to engage in political activity in the name of the *Risale-i Nur* movement. Nursi merely saw the Democrats as a party that would take a firm stand against communism and irreligion; he even described Adnan Menderes, the Prime Minister of the time, as a 'champion of Islam'. His support for the Democrat Party included his voting for them in the elections of 1957.

Nursi also placed great importance on re-establishing and strengthening relations with the rest of the Muslim world during this final period of his life. For example, he applauded the Democrat Government's decision to sign the Baghdad Pact between Turkey and Iraq, subsequently joined by Pakistan, Iran, and Britain in 1955, seeing this as an important step in promoting peace in the area, particularly among Muslim countries. His support for the government's decisions to establish good relations with neighbouring Muslim states continued throughout the rest of his life (Vahide, *Intellectual Biography*, 53–5, 331).

Before concluding this section there is one more event worthy of mention. During the 1950s, the *Risale-i Nur* attracted numerous new students and readers in many different parts of the world:

> The last section of Nursi's 'official' biography, published during his lifetime in 1958, is devoted to these developments and includes letters from *Risale-i Nur* students from as far afield as Finland and Washington, as well as various Islamic countries. (Vahide, *Intellectual Biography*, 343)

Nursi sent a number of students abroad to spread the message of the *Risale-i Nur*, to countries such as Germany, Pakistan, Syria and Korea. He sent copies of the work to a number of foreign countries, including Germany, Finland, America, Japan, India, Indonesia, Egypt and some African countries. Nursi believed in the co-operation of Muslims and sincere Christians in the face of aggressive atheism. He sent a copy of the *Risale* to the Pope and received a letter of thanks from the Vatican, dated 22 February 1951.[6] He also visited the Greek Orthodox Patriarch of Istanbul, Patriarch Athenagoras, in the spring and summer of 1953. Nursi also received visits from a number of important religious scholars and figures from various parts of the Muslim world.

It was during this period that the *Risale-i Nur* began to be printed on modern presses in the Latin alphabet. Thousands of copies of the work were printed and sent to various places in Anatolia. In 1953, a book entitled *A Key to the World of the*

---

[6] Bediüzzaman Said Nursi, 'Emirdağ Lâhikası – 2', in *Risale-i Nur Külliyatı*, 1834.

Risale-i Nur was published, consisting of the letters written while Nursi was in Isparta and Istanbul. Nursi attached great importance to translations, both of the original Turkish into Arabic – to spread the *Risale-i Nur* throughout the wider Islamic world – and of the Arabic parts of the work into Turkish. He himself translated *The Damascus Sermon* into Turkish in 1951, while his younger brother Abdülmecid, who was then mufti of Ürgüp near Kayseri, translated *The Staff of Moses* collection into Arabic at Bediüzzaman's suggestion. Nursi wanted to interest as many people as possible in his work. In 1955, Abdülmecid translated both *İşârâtü' l-İ'câz* (The Signs of Miraculousness), the Qur'anic commentary written by Bediüzzaman during the First World War, and his *Mesnevî-i Nuriye* from Arabic into Turkish. The Turkish translation of *İşârâtü'l-İ'câz* was then printed in Ankara in the new alphabet.

The increasing availability of the *Risale-i Nur* led to a considerable increase in the number of students and, concomitantly, the opening of numerous *Risale* study centres (*dershanes*) through the length and breadth of Turkey.[7]

Finally, when he died, Nursi was renowned as the founder of the most powerful text-based faith movement in Turkey, with the number of Nurcu students estimated at more than one and a half million. Despite a life characterized by strife, hardship and adversity, Nursi arguably changed the face of Turkish Islam forever, leaving a body of work that continues to inspire millions of people across the Muslim world and beyond, and standing shoulder to shoulder with the most influential Muslims scholars and philosophers of the twentieth century.

---

[7] Vahide, 'The Life and Times of Bediüzzaman Said Nursi', 243.

THE *RISALE-I NUR*: LANGUAGE AND STRUCTURE

Nursi wrote largely in Ottoman Turkish, although some of the separate treatises which make up the *Risale-i Nur* were originally penned in Arabic. There are also a number of passages composed in Persian, with which he was familiar. His language is that of the classical Muslim orators: a florid, rhetorical language that is highly metaphorical and often quite elusive to all but the most trained reader. Although the new generation of Nurcus continue to call on the elders of the Nur community to sanction editing of the *Risale-i Nur* in order to make it more linguistically accessible to the masses, the elders have resisted, arguing that the original should be kept as Nursi himself wished.

With the individual treatises which comprise the work described variously as 'rays', 'gleams' and 'flashes', the *Risale* models itself as a sort of hermeneutical prism, catching what its author considers to be the effulgence of divine light from the Qur'an and refracting it as colours visible to, and understandable by, the eye of the human heart. Inspired by the sense of drama which underpins the landscaping of his work, we suggest that we approach the *Risale* as one would a building. In fact, the *Risale* is not one building, but a whole complex of edifices, constructed at various points along the author's career. In the West it remains largely unknown, although there have been attempts in recent years to excavate, rather as one would some fabulous desert palace, lost for years beneath the sands and uncovered gradually, brick by brick. As such, the complex is largely intact. True, the earlier structures – those which date to Nursi's formative period, when the self-styled 'Old Said' was by his own admission preoccupied with the natural sciences and speculative philosophy – are showing signs of wear and tear. The more recent additions to the complex, however, are as impressive now as they must have been when first erected. Nevertheless, many of the buildings which make up the complex remain unexplored, and even those which have been open to the public for years contain rooms, passages and tunnels that remain locked to this day.

While the extended analogy of the *Risale* as a complex of buildings may seem little more than a decorative literary conceit, it is not without utility. It is in keeping with Nursi's own extensive and often flamboyant use of allegory and metaphor, and reminds us that he was first and foremost a communicator, with a communicator's sense of what best facilitates understanding of the message being communicated. It also conveys something of the unity of composition and design which underpins the *Risale*, with each of its component structures adding strength and sense of purpose to the other, while contributing to a whole that is most definitely more than just the sum of its parts.

3

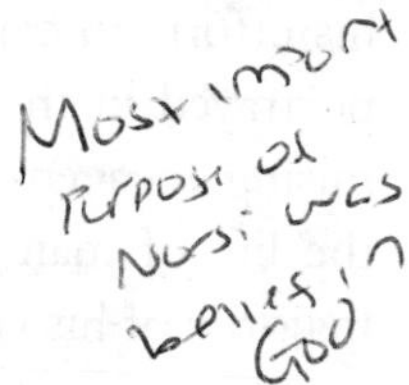

Thought and teachings

THE PRIMACY OF BELIEF

For Nursi, the most important objective of his endeavours was the safeguarding and strengthening of belief in God, which for him was the beating heart of religion and the cement which holds human society together. He lived at a time when religious conviction was under severe attack from the encroachment of what he believed to be alien ideologies, the cumulative effect of which had been to erode the collective faith of the Muslim world and catapult the unwary among the Muslims into the ambit of materialism and secularity. However, the fault did not lie solely with forces outside the Muslim world: Muslims themselves had increasingly become habituated to imitative (*taqlīdī*) belief, blindly emulating their forebears and failing to think for themselves. Nursi wished to strengthen the faith of his Muslim brethren by transforming it from pure imitation into belief based on investigation (*taḥqīq*) and conviction. In order to do this, he maintained, the fundamentals of belief (*uṣūl al-īmān*) had to be emphasized above all other considerations. Rather than spend his energies on expounding the finer points of jurisprudence or campaigning for the reestablishment of the Caliphate and the revival of the *shari'a*, Nursi devoted all of his efforts to expounding the truths and realities of belief as portrayed in the Qur'an. It is his relentless and uncompromising engagement with the issue of belief and its primacy in the life of man that distinguishes Said Nursi from the vast majority of his contemporaries.

According to Nursi, there is a pressing need to explain to modern man the basic tenets of the Qur'an – the unity of God; prophethood; and the existence of the Hereafter – in such a way that both heart and intellect are satisfied. For Nursi, these truths provide the only answer to the existential dilemma facing all human beings: Who am I? Where am I from? What must I do here? Where am I going? What will happen when I die? The cultivation of belief, he said, was the only antidote to the terror which man faces when he is unable to answer that existential dilemma to his satisfaction. He wrote:

> If luminaries such as Shaykh 'Abd al-Qadir Jilani, Shah Naqshband and Imam-i Rabbani were alive today, they would expend all their efforts in strengthening the truths of belief and tenets of Islam. For they are the means to eternal happiness. If there is deficiency in them, it results in eternal misery. A person without belief may not enter Paradise, but very many have gone to Paradise without Sufism. Man cannot live without bread, but he can live without fruit. Sufism is the fruit, the truths of Islam, basic sustenance. In former times, through spiritual journeying from forty days to as much as forty years, a person might rise to some of the truths of belief. But now, if through Almighty God's mercy there is a way to rise to those truths in forty minutes, it surely is not sensible to remain indifferent to it. (*The Letters*, transl. Vahide , 41)

Nursi's aim was thus to expound and disseminate the truths of the Qur'an and engender a 'culture of belief' upon which modern and successful society might base itself.

Nursi's thoughts on the necessity of belief did not of course develop in a vacuum, and both his message and his methodology were informed by the socio-political and cultural context in which he found himself. As we have seen earlier, Nursi's life coincided with a period of great change in the Muslim world, with the rise of new ideologies and belief systems which, combined with the cultural and political hegemony of the West, had dealt a body blow to religious faith across the whole Muslim world. These changes occurred thanks to the establishment of direct imperial control of Muslim countries through the formation of new, Western-oriented, nationalistic state-systems. Materialism and communism were at their peak and the world appeared to be in psycho-spiritual crisis. Momentous advances in the field of the natural sciences were used in some quarters as a stick to beat religion, creating doubts about their most cherished beliefs in the minds of Christians, Jews and Muslims alike. Ashur writes:

> The sciences, which are reconciled with Islam, were deliberately being used against it. They were endeavouring to show that Islam, the religion of civilization, was opposed to progress and technology. (Ashur, 'Bediüzzaman's Defence Strategy', 232)

Society had begun to embrace multiple gods, hiding them under the umbrella of ideologies such as atheism or existentialism:

> And certainly many philosophers have worshipped gods in some form. Rijson saw life itself as a god, while Darwin deified evolution. Hegel thought the absolute spirit was god, while Marx recognized dialectic materialism as god. Others are society, which Durkheim deified; sexuality, which Freud deified; the individual, which Sartre

made into a false god. All these are nothing other than names given to acts and events pertaining to society, life, man, and the universe, which God has created. (Ubayd, 'Methods of Teaching in the *Risale-i Nur*', 250)

The Darwinistic view, for example, implied that human moral nature and religion had both evolved naturalistically: now there was no need for a God or religion to explain life. Darwinism contradicted some ideas in the Scriptures and was viewed as a threat to revealed religions. Sigmund Freud, on the other hand, considered sex as being at the heart of the personality, and that civilization depends on the sublimation of sexual energy. Although philosophers, psychologists and artists increasingly became aware of the basic problem of modern humanity, namely that faith had been lost, they were unable to identify anything substantial that might replace it. Titus Burckhardt summarized the argument thus:

The sun-centred system bears a clear symbolism, for it situates the light-source at the centre. However, Copernicus' rediscovery of this system did not bring any new spiritual view. It was in fact the popularization of an esoteric truth to a dangerous extent. The sun-centred system has no shared aspect with people's subjective experiences. Religious belief has no organic place in this system. In place of pointing out to man's intellect the ways it could surpass itself and ensuring the evaluating of everything within the extraordinariness of the cosmos, it merely opened up the way to a materialist Prometheanism which was not even human, let alone superhuman. (Burckhardt, *Cosmology and Modern Science*, 184–5, cited in Kıllıoğlu, 'The Concept of the "I" in [Nursi's] Works', 284)

The world in general, and the new Turkish Republic in particular, were in the grip of socio-psychological depression. Until then, the revealed religions had had a great effect on all kind of relations, from governmental to societal, but now a new 'religion' had appeared, declaring that there was no need for messages or moral precepts emanating from beyond the confines of the visible world. For some, man was now deeply mired in spiritual crisis and alienation, having lost his centre and become a mere physical arena for the fulfilment of economic or sexual aims. Erich Fromm defined the problem of modernity as follows:

> Christianity has preached spiritual renewal, neglecting the changes in the social order without which spiritual renewal must remain ineffective for the majority of the people. The age of enlightenment has postulated as the highest norms independent judgement and reason; it preached political equality without seeing that political equality could not lead to the realization of the brotherhood of man if it was not accompanied by a fundamental change in the social-economic organization. Socialism, and especially Marxism, has stressed the necessity for social and economic changes, and neglected the necessity of the inner change in human beings, without which economic change can never lead to the 'good society'. (Fromm, *The Sane Society*, 272)

Karl Popper, writing about the rise of imperialism after the Industrial Revolution, believed that

> ... the Naturalist revolt against God, which preceded the historians' revolt, replaced God with Nature. Apart from this, almost everything remained the same. Naturalism replaced theology, natural laws replaced Divine laws, natural will and power (the forces of Nature) replaced Divine will and power, and finally Natural Selection replaced the Divine order and judgement. Naturalist determinism replaced theological determinism, that is, Nature's being omnipotent and omniscient replaced God's being omnipotent and omniscient. (Bolay, 'Bediüzzaman's View of Philosophy', 254)

The appearance of Nursi's ideas coincided with a proliferation of materialist writing in the late Ottoman Empire. Subsequent to the Tanzimat, various political, literary and philosophical ideologies had begun to flow in from abroad, impacting considerably on Ottoman intellectual life. Among these, materialism, positivism, Darwinism, Freudianism,

naturalism, socialism and atheism left profound negative effects on many Ottoman intellectuals. Muslim scholars reacted in various ways, but mostly through ill-conceived refutations or rebuttals unsubstantiated by rational evidence.

After the foundation of the Turkish Republic, materialism, Freudianism and existentialism made their influence felt on the policy makers of the new state, who attributed Turkey's problems to Islam without realizing that Western man was also in spiritual crisis. For the Ottoman modernists it was Islam and the Islamic way of life that were deemed responsible for centuries of backwardness and lack of development in science and technology. There was only one solution: Islam had to be removed from social, public and political structures. After the collapse of the Ottomans and the foundation of the Turkish Republic, religion was duly excised from public life, while 'positivist-materialism', secularism and atheism gradually began to take root:

> It was a period in which every sort of religious enterprise was labelled 'a reactionary movement'; religiously minded people who performed worship even privately were disturbed; when both reading and teaching the Qur'an were forbidden; blameless religious scholars were sent to the scaffold due to unfounded suspicions; and severe penalties were inflicted for the teaching of religion. Yes, it was a time when the religious schools and Sufi meeting-places were closed down, which for hundreds of years had been the watchmen of this nation's spiritual life, honour, and all they hold sacred; when anywhere thought to be a place of religious learning was extinguished; when all religious instruction was prohibited; and when some shaykhs and religious scholars were intimidated into 'selling themselves' and accepting various positions… (Aydüz, 'Guidance and Tebliğ in the *Risale-i Nur*', 190)

As Şerif Mardin points out (*Religion and Social Change*, 169), the secularizing reform movements of the Ottoman Empire, and later the Turkish Republic, had served to create a disconnected society. Educational reforms neglected rural communities, in which for centuries Islam had occupied a central place. Such conditions presented Nursi with a golden opportunity in which to develop his discourse and aim to reconstruct society on the foundations of true belief in the Qur'an. Mardin concludes that the secular primary education in the Republican educational system, which recognized no place for religion, and which was based on a positivistic world view, was totally at odds with the moral universe of Islam, and that Nursi was provided with fertile ground on which to sow his ideas concerning the total involvement of the individual in Islam.

THE CENTRAL THEMES OF THE *RISALE-I NUR*

To identify the major themes of Nursi's *magnum opus*, the 5000-page *Risale-i Nur*, is no easy task. The scope of this book means that it is impossible to cover everything and so, notwithstanding the fact that singling out one theme rather than another will always be invidious, we have to limit our choice to the overarching themes upon which, we believe, the *Risale* is constructed. There are six of them, and they, in no particular order, are as follows.

(i) Nursi and 'the most beautiful names'

Running like a thread throughout Nursi's writings is his uncompromisingly theocentric portrayal of the cosmos as a divinely-penned 'book', comprised of 'words' or 'verses' which, once deconstructed, are revealed as nothing less than embodiments or individuations of the 'beautiful names' (*asmā al-ḥusnā*) of God Himself. Nursi's view of creation is thus a wholly sacramental one, in which the transcendent sacred – the Divine – imbues all things.

That God possesses innumerable 'beautiful names', and not just the ninety-nine mentioned in the *ḥadīth* or counted on the rosary, is nothing new in the theology of Islam. Emphasis on the centrality of the divine attributes of perfection clearly originates in Qur'anic passages which enumerate the divine bounties, or which describe the workings of God in the world and end invariably in the mention of one or more of the Divine names. Acknowledgement of the utter indebtedness of the cosmos to the 'manifestation' of those names appeared relatively early on in Muslim liturgy, finding particular resonance in the invocations of the Prophet and his household. In the *Invocation of Kumayl*, for example, taught by 'Ali b. Abi Talib to one of his disciples, we read that 'the beautiful names of God are the pillars which hold up all things', while countless supplications attributed to the Imams of the Alid line are constructed around the names and attributes of God. Later, of course, meditation upon the names of God became a staple of Sufi literature, with whole cosmologies founded on the premise of 'manifestation' and the created world as 'mirror' for the reflection of the Divine. Nursi's view of the cosmos as a multiplicity of loci for the ceaseless and ever-changing manifestation of the divine names is to an extent informed by the teachings of a number of major gnostic thinkers, including Ibn ʿArabī and Imam Aḥmad Sirhindī, although the literary and didactic means he employs to articulate it are undoubtedly his own.

In the Nursian scheme, the visible realm (*'ālam al-shahāda*) is akin to a full-length mirror in which the 'hidden treasure' that is God manifests Himself in order to contemplate His own perfection. While on the level of divine essence, this act of contemplation is self-reflexive, on the level of divine acts, contemplation is mediated through creation, at the pinnacle of which stands man. For Nursi, all created beings manifest God's names to some degree: the whole of the cosmos becomes a hierophany, with each created being hymning the praises of God through its innate disposition. However, unlike Eliade's perception of the hierophanic, which posits each of the constituent beings in the cosmos as *potentially* indicative of the sacred, Nursi's vision is one in which all things *actually* and *actively* reflect the Other, yet without compromising their own distinct otherness. Acutely aware that the perception of the world as God's personal mirror may tempt some to dismiss the created realm as a phantasm and declare, along with some of the more extremist advocates of 'unity of being' (*waḥdat al-wujūd*), that 'all is God', Nursi is at pains to draw clear lines of distinction between his own schema and that of the pantheists. Nursi's delicate balancing act, in which he juggles the declaration of God's incomparability (*tanzīh*) with that of His similarity (*tashbīh*), serves to ensure on the one hand that in His immanence, God is not confused with His creation, and on the other hand that in His transcendence, He is not seen as absent or unconcerned with the day-to-day workings of the cosmos.

Nursi also devotes huge swathes of the *Risale* to eloquent expositions of the 'book of Creation' – *kitâb-ı kâinat* – in which all of God's 'words' – expressions of His attributes – are written for all to read. Man's understanding of God is thus posited as experiential, for everyone is tasked with the interpretation of the same cosmic text, in which the attributes of perfection are made manifest for all to ponder. Yet while all read, only some come to the desired conclusion. For Nursi, it is only by pondering the countless divine names made manifest in the created realm, with their seemingly numberless permutations and gradations, that man, using his own receptivity to the attributes of perfection, is able to reach the truth of belief and fulfil his true destiny, which is to act as a conscious mirror for the reflection of his Creator:

Now the true meaning of your life is this: its acting as a mirror to the manifestation of Divine oneness and the manifestation of the Eternally Besought One. That is to say, through a comprehensiveness as though being the point of focus for all the Divine Names manifested in the world, it is its being a mirror to the Single and Eternally Besought One. (*The Words*, transl. Vahide, 141)

For Nursi, the key to belief consists, *inter alia*, of deciphering the signs which exist 'in the self and on the horizons' (Qur'an, 41. 53) in order to unlock the talisman of creation and reveal the true worth of man, which is his position as vicegerent of God. By knowing what he is, and, more importantly, what he is not, he can, to paraphrase the words of the *ḥadīth*, come to know his Lord.[1] From the Nursian perspective, the attainment of belief, and the strengthening of belief once it is attained, is contingent upon man's ability to read the cosmic text 'in the name of God' or *bismillah* – a phrase which he must assimilate into his consciousness if he is to sustain the vicegerency entrusted to him:

Yes, this phrase is a treasury so blessed that your infinite impotence and poverty bind you to an infinite power and mercy; it makes your impotence and poverty a most acceptable intercessor at the Court of One All-Powerful and Compassionate. The person who acts saying, 'In the Name of God', resembles someone who enrols in the army. He acts in the name of the government; he has fear of no-one; he speaks, performs every matter, and withstands everything in the name of the law and the name of the government. (*The Words*, transl. Vahide, 16)

---

[1] 'Whosoever knows his own self, knows his Lord' [*Man 'arafa nafsahu qad 'arafa rabbahu*] is a staple of Naqshbandi thought, and claimed to have been influential on Nursi in his formative years. Note, however, that the authenticity of this tradition is contested by many mainstream Sunni scholars.

Nursi's portrayal of the cosmos as a vast 'book' replete with signs (*āyāt*) for man to decipher complements the Qur'an's own portrayal of itself as a book replete with verses (*āyāt*) which describe and point to its Author. The intertextuality of the 'revealed Book' that is the Qur'an and the 'created book' that is the cosmos was clearly not lost on the author of the *Risale*, who on numerous occasions alludes to their complementary relationship. Nursi often uses the term 'Book of Creation' or 'cosmic book' (*kitâb-ı kâinat*) to describe the created realm, but on several occasions goes so far as to describe the universe almost as a kind of *über*-Qur'an, as in the phrase '...the mighty Qur'an inscribed by Divine power and called the universe...' (*The Words*, transl. Vahide, 484).

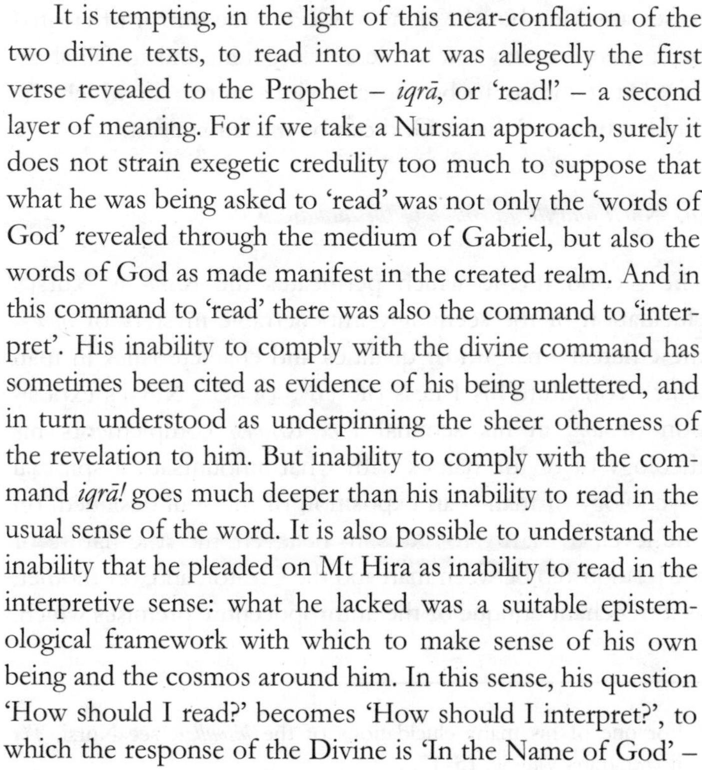

It is tempting, in the light of this near-conflation of the two divine texts, to read into what was allegedly the first verse revealed to the Prophet – *iqrā*, or 'read!' – a second layer of meaning. For if we take a Nursian approach, surely it does not strain exegetic credulity too much to suppose that what he was being asked to 'read' was not only the 'words of God' revealed through the medium of Gabriel, but also the words of God as made manifest in the created realm. And in this command to 'read' there was also the command to 'interpret'. His inability to comply with the divine command has sometimes been cited as evidence of his being unlettered, and in turn understood as underpinning the sheer otherness of the revelation to him. But inability to comply with the command *iqrā!* goes much deeper than his inability to read in the usual sense of the word. It is also possible to understand the inability that he pleaded on Mt Hira as inability to read in the interpretive sense: what he lacked was a suitable epistemological framework with which to make sense of his own being and the cosmos around him. In this sense, his question 'How should I read?' becomes 'How should I interpret?', to which the response of the Divine is 'In the Name of God' –

interpret the cosmos as a manifestation of One Who created you; interpret it as a vast book, replete with Signs which point to Me. For Nursi, the words *'bismillāh al-raḥmān al-raḥīm'* are more than just a formula that, in Muslim tradition, is prescribed before the performance of certain actions: it indicates an epistemological framework for Qur'anic theology that was possibly in place from the outset of the Prophetic mission, and which informs most of the popular theology in the *Risale*.[2]

For Nursi, then, man is truly fulfilled only with the attainment of belief, and belief is contingent on the correct interpretation of the cosmic narrative: to read anything but the words of God inscribed on the pages of the universe, or to see anything but the signs of God in the mirror of created beings, is to betray one's role as vicegerent and to fall short of what it means to be the conscious mirror in which the 'hidden treasure' that is God can be made manifest.

(ii) Nursi and the talisman of the human 'I'

The second theme which permeates the *Risale* is Nursi's elucidation of the seemingly impenetrable mystery of *anā* – the ethereal amalgam of qualities and characteristics in man which constitute his I-ness or sense of self. Nursi's exposition of *anā* in his seminal *Ene Risalesi* complements his theology of divine names with what amounts to a spiritual psychology of man – an exposition of the soul designed, on one level, to clarify for Muslim believers the true nature of the relationship between man and the Creator, and, on another, as a trenchant critique of the anthropocentric premises which,

---

2 For one of his many elucidations of the *bismillah*, see Nursi, *The Words*, trans Vahide, 15–17.

he claims, underpin both classical philosophy and the whole project of modernity. As such, it is arguably the key theme of Nursian thought.

In deconstructing this *anā*, this '*alif* from the book of the character of mankind' (*The Words*, trans Vahide, 550), which owns nothing yet claims everything, Nursi shows what happens when man tries to wear the 'clothes of God', unaware that they neither suit nor fit him. For every soul, he asserts, possesses the wherewithal to appreciate, receive and reflect the names of God. Yet if the connection between man and God is severed, man appropriates the attributes of perfection for himself, believing erroneously that he is the owner of all that he has, and all that he is. Rather than 'give back' or 'surrender' these attributes by reflecting them 'in God's Name', he keeps them for himself and attempts to augment and perfect them, not by manifesting God but by acting as though he himself were worthy of worship. Indeed, in order to be able to consider his attributes his own, he must constantly bow down before others and acknowledge them as masters of their own fate, even if this means abasing himself before them.

The divine 'trust'

The ability of each human individual to talk about him or herself as 'I', Nursi contends, was given to man as part of the Divine 'trust'.

> We did indeed offer the Trust to the Heavens and the Earth and the Mountains; but they refused to undertake it, being afraid thereof: but man undertook it – he was indeed unjust and foolish. (Qur'an, 33. 72)

A 'trust' is something that is given to an individual, and over which he has power of disposal: he is expected to use it in the manner prescribed by the giver of the trust, although he also has the power to go against the giver's wishes and dispose of the trust in any way that he likes. In the context of the Creator–creature relationship, what is this 'trust' that man agreed to take upon himself, after cosmic phenomena such as the heavens and the mountains had refused it? Nursi is not alone in defining the 'trust' as man's God-given ability to act as divine 'vicegerent'; in accepting the 'trust', man takes it upon himself to act as God's 'representative' on earth.

To understand exactly what the Nursian conception of 'representing' God entails, we have to look to those verses in the Qur'an which refer to the creation of mankind. Several passages discuss the drama of man's first appearance on the cosmic stage, but none is quite so succinct as the account given in verses 30 to 40 of the second *sūra*, *al-Baqara*.

> Your Lord said to the angels: 'I will create a vicegerent on earth.' They said: 'Will You place therein one who will make mischief therein and shed blood – while we do celebrate Your praises and glorify Your holy (name)?' He said: 'I know what you do not know.' And He taught Adam the names of all things; then He placed them before the angels, and said: 'Tell me the names of these if you are right.' They said: 'Glory to You, of knowledge We have none, save what You have taught us. In truth it is You Who are perfect in knowledge and wisdom.' He said: 'O Adam! Tell them their names.' When he had told them, God said: 'Did I not tell you that I know the secrets of heaven and earth, and I know what you reveal and what you conceal?' And We said to the angels: 'Bow down to Adam.' (Qur'an, 2. 30–4)

The key which unlocks the meaning of this passage lies in the 'names' which God 'taught' to Adam, who as the 'first man' represents the totality of humankind. For Nursi, like other gnostic thinkers in the Muslim tradition, the names taught by God to man are none other than the 'beautiful names' of God Himself. In imparting knowledge of His names, not only does God teach man to recognize all of the divine attributes of perfection, but He also gives him the ability to display those attributes consciously and, in so doing, act as God's 'representative' on earth. In other words, man is able to recognize divine attributes of perfection such as power, wisdom, mercy, beauty and the like simply by virtue of the fact that he is, in one sense, created in God's image.

It is on account of man's potential to act as God's representative that the angels were asked to acknowledge man's creational status by 'bowing down' to him. In the cosmology of the Qur'an, angels are endowed with limited knowledge of God's names, and while they worship God with perfect sincerity and awareness, they do so lacking the free will to disobey. Man, on the other hand, is endowed not only with knowledge of all of God's names, but also with free will: if man uses his knowledge of the names wisely and bows down to God of his own volition, he rises above the angels and fulfils his destiny as the jewel in the crown of creation. However, if he abuses his knowledge of the names and fails to fulfil his part of the 'trust', he sinks to a position described by the Qur'an as the 'lowest of the low'.

The 'trust', then, offers whoever accepts it the ability to know God and to 'experience' Him through His 'beautiful names' and attributes of perfection. But whoever accepts a trust must also undertake the responsibility to dispose of what he is given in accordance with the wishes of the giver: should he discharge his responsibility successfully, he will reap the reward; should he fail, he must face the consequences. In the context of the trust offered by God, the responsibility is a momentous one, for what it actually means in practice is assuming the attributes of God and acting not only in His name, but in complete accordance with His will. It is only when man grasps the significance of the trust and what it means in practice to accept such an undertaking that he can see why cosmic phenomena such as the heavens and the mountains – both symbols of might and grandeur – refused the challenge.

The function of the human 'I'

The 'I', then, is considered by Nursi to be part of the trust given to man by God. The 'I', he goes on to say, is not only the means through which we are able to understand the 'names' of God, but it is also the 'key to the locked talisman of creation'. When we understand the meaning of 'I', Nursi assures us, the locked doors of creation will open and the riddle of cosmic existence will be solved. The ability of the 'I' – the self – to know God stems from its containing within itself what Nursi calls 'indications and samples' which reflect the attributes and functions of God. In this sense, the 'I' is like a unit of measurement which exists solely for the sake of revealing the existence and measure of something else. Like any other unit of measurement, the 'I' does not have a concrete material existence:

> It is not necessary for a unit of measurement to have actual existence. Rather, like hypothetical lines in geometry, a unit of measurement may be formed by hypothesis and supposition. It is not necessary for its actual existence to be established by concrete knowledge and proofs. (Nursi, *Man and the Universe*, 22)

Whether the 'I' is part of the soul or the spirit, or it is a function of the conscience or the psyche, Nursi never elucidates. What is clear, however, is that the 'I' is an abstract entity whose sole function is to act as a kind of yardstick against which God's names can be 'measured'. Such a yardstick is necessary, it would seem, because in dealing with God we are dealing with a being Who is absolute and all-encompassing. The fact that something is absolute and all-encompassing, without shape or form, means that under normal circumstances it cannot be perceived. If the whole of the cosmos were coloured red, we would be unable to perceive it, simply because there would be nothing against which red might be compared and thus distinguished: if everything were red, we would not be able to perceive it as such. Nursi uses the example of endless light to elucidate his argument:

> For example, an endless light without darkness may not be known or perceived. But if a line of real or imaginary darkness is drawn, it [i.e. the light] then becomes known. (Nursi, *Man and the Universe*, 22)

Light is discernible only because it exists in degrees. In other words, without the existence of darkness, light would remain imperceptible. Darkness is needed in order to reveal or render perceptible the existence of light. In that sense, it is, like the human 'I', a yardstick. And, like the human 'I', darkness has no concrete material existence. Darkness is simply an absence of light: in and of itself it does not exist.

The yardstick of the human 'I' is needed, then, because the attributes and names of God, such as knowledge, power, mercy, compassion and wisdom, are all-encompassing, limitless and without like. In order to discern them, man must impose on them an imaginary limit, like the line of darkness that is used to make known the light. This imaginary limit is placed on the Divine attributes of perfection by the human 'I'.

How the 'I' does this, Nursi contends, is perfectly simple: it imagines that it is the owner of its own self. In other words, it claims ownership over all of the attributes of perfection that it experiences as part of its own existence. The human self looks at the power, beauty, wisdom, compassion and knowledge within its own being and claims to be the owner of them all. This ownership appears to be very real, but, as Nursi argues, it is illusory, its function being simply to reveal or indicate the true Owner of the attribute:

> For example, with its imagined dominicality over what it owns, the 'I' may understand the dominicality of its Creator over contingent creation. And with its apparent ownership, it may understand the true ownership of its Creator, saying, 'Just as I am the owner of this house, so too is the Creator the owner of this creation.' (Nursi, *Man and the Universe*, 23)

Similarly, through his own knowledge, man may understand the knowledge of God; through his own art, man may understand the art of the Creator, and so on. Man looks at his own creative powers and extrapolates from them, concluding that whoever or whatever is responsible for creation of the universe must possess similar powers, but on a truly cosmic scale. At this embryonic stage of man's spiritual journey, he 'shares' the attributes between himself and God, reasoning that since he has power, God too must have power, but on a scale befitting God; the same applies to all of the divine attributes of perfection.

According to Nursi, the 'I', then, is nothing but a mirror-like unit of measurement, or a tool, through which man is able to discover the Creator: it has no meaning in itself, and exists only to reveal the existence and meaning of the absolute. However, as Nursi points out, the 'I' is a double-edged sword, for while it is designed to lead man to God, if misunderstood it may lead man in the other direction.

If man uses his 'I' to journey towards God, at some stage – either through his own reasoning or through the grace of revelation – he will realize that only One Who is absolute in every sense of the word can be creator and nurturer of the cosmos. In other words, those attributes of perfection that the 'I' was once content to 'share' conceptually between itself and God now have to be 'surrendered' in their entirety to God alone, whose possession of such attributes must, of necessity, be absolute.

But where does this leave human attributes? Nursi argues that man's power is imaginary: the ownership he appears to exercise over his attributes is an illusion, there only to reveal the very real and absolute attributes of man's Maker. Realization of this truth is, according to Nursi, the kernel of real worship and true submission:

> That is to say, the 'I' [...] realizes that it serves one other than itself. Its essence has only an indicative meaning. That is, it understands that it carries the meaning of another. Its existence is dependent; that is, it believes that its existence is due only to the existence of another, and that the continuance of its existence is due solely to the creativity of that other. Its ownership is illusory; that is, it knows that with the permission of its owner it has an apparent and temporary ownership. (Nursi, *Man and the Universe*, 29)

The submission of 'I'

The issue of 'ownership' is key here, for it is the metaphorical 'surrender' of man's temporary and illusory ownership over his own attributes that underpins the notion of *islām* or submission. For it is only by 'giving up' one's claims to ownership of one's attributes that one can begin to comprehend the idea of 'purification of the self', which lies at the heart of Qur'anic – and, by extension, Nursian – spirituality.

True 'surrender' is only possible if the 'I' is realized for what it is, namely a nebulous, insubstantial mechanism that exists solely to indicate its Creator. Once it has truly accepted this, the 'I' will abandon its imaginary ownership and admit that all attributes belong to God alone. It will realize that whatever it appears to 'own' is there in the form of a loan, to be 'given back' to its rightful Owner. To 'give back' the attributes means to use them in a manner dictated by the One who gave them in the first place. To submit one's (imaginary) knowledge, for example, means to nurture it for God's sake and to use it in accordance with His will alone. It also means to attribute it to Him at all times and in all circumstances, and not to appropriate it for oneself or to imagine that one has any real power of disposal over it. Submission involves the conscious attribution of all of the attributes of perfection to God, thus turning the self quite consciously into a mirror through which God's attributes can be reflected for others to see. The surrendered *anā* forms the basis of what Nursi calls 'the line of prophethood' – the current of thought which bases itself on a reading of the cosmic narrative mediated through acceptance of Divine sovereignty.

The unregenerate 'I'

The alternative, as Nursi points out, is for the 'I' within man to hold onto its illusory ownership and deny that there is a Creator with greater claim to sovereignty. This happens when the 'I' fails or refuses to recognize its true function and sees itself solely in the light of its nominal and apparent meaning. If the 'I' believes that it owns itself, it cannot act consciously and sincerely as the vicegerent of God, and thus fails the trust.

For Nursi, it is not difficult to understand why an 'I' would choose the path of self-assertion rather than self-submission. If man is created in God's image, with small 'samples' or 'reflections' of the Divine attributes deposited in his innermost being in order to allow him to recognize God, is it surprising that he should want to claim these attributes as his own? When one is so used to power, wisdom, beauty and the like, to be told that they belong elsewhere and must be 'surrendered' is to invite incredulity, often followed by rebellion and denial. The longer that the 'I' claims ownership, the more difficult it will become to submit. Eventually, the 'I' swells, puffed up by its imaginary sovereignty, until it transforms the person into a creature that is propelled purely by considerations of 'self'. Rather than using the 'I' as a yardstick to indicate God, it begins to measure all other things against itself, and becomes the centre of its own universe. It is the unregenerate *anā* which fuels what Nursi calls 'the line of philosophy', which is the outcome of man's attempt to read the cosmic narrative through the prism of his own self, without reference to God. As such, it is completely antithetical to the 'line of prophethood', as mentioned earlier.

Furthermore, in order to retain the ownership it believes it exercises over its attributes, it begins to 'divide' the absolute sovereignty of God between itself and other beings. Instead of attributing power to God, for example, it attributes it to nature, to causes, and to other beings. As Nursi puts it:

> It is just like a man who steals a brass coin from the public treasury: he can only justify his actions by agreeing to take a silver coin for each of his friends that is present. So the man who says, 'I own myself', must believe and say, 'Everything owns itself'. (Nursi, *Man and the Universe*, 263)

Therein lies the way of *shirk*, or the ascription to God of 'partners' – the cardinal, unforgivable sin that the heavens and the mountains were terrified of committing should they accept the trust and fail.

Nursi's exposition of *anā*, outlining as it does his perspective on the Qur'anic spiritual psychology of man, is key to the spiritual character of the *Risale*, yet remains virtually unexplored by Western writers.

(iii) The 'self-referential' and the 'Other-indicative'

The third theme is Nursi's elucidation of the twin concepts of *ma'nā-i ismī* and *ma'nā-i ḥarfī*, representing the two diametrically opposed hermeneutical positions open to man as 'reader' of the cosmic narrative. For Nursi, the polarity is stark and simple: either one interprets the individual verses in the cosmic narrative as 'Other-indicative' (*ma'nā-i ḥarfī*), namely as signs pointing to the Creator; or one uproots them from their Divine origin and imposes on them a 'self-referential' meaning (*ma'nā-i ismī*), claiming that they indicate none other than their own existences. To grasp the dynamics of Nursi's treatment of *ismī* and *ḥarfī* 'meanings' allows us insights into his approach to the sacred/profane dichotomy, and provides us, *inter alia*, with a fresh understanding of *ḥayāt al-dunyā*. In the Qur'an there are 64 occurrences of this phrase (see, for example, 7. 51 or 46. 20), indicating what is, on one level, the complete antithesis of Qur'anic spirituality as adumbrated by Bediüzzaman.

Arguably the most salient example of the *ismī/ḥarfī* polarity used by Nursi appears toward the end of the 'First Principle' of the 'Twelfth Word', where he juxtaposes the Qur'anic view of the cosmos with the view espoused by 'natural philo-sophy' or 'science':

> Yes, the All-Wise Qur'an… regards beings, each of which is a meaningful letter, as bearing the meaning of another, that is, it looks at them on account of their Maker. It says, 'How beautifully they have been made! How exquisitely they point to their Maker's beauty!', thus showing the universe's true beauty. But the philosophy they call natural philosophy or science has plunged into the decorations of the letters of beings and into their relationships, and has become bewildered; it has confused the way of reality. While the letters of this mighty book should be looked at as *bearing the meaning of another*, that is, on account of God, they have not done this; they have looked at beings as *signifying themselves*… (*The Words*, transl. Vahide, 145; italics added)

For Nursi, interpretation of the constituents of the cosmos as self-referential is a corollary of the skewed epistemological framework imposed on creation by the unregenerate *anā*, and which underpins the endeavours characterized by the 'line of philosophy'. In contradistinction to this, an interpretation of the cosmos that is mediated by revelation will see all things as being 'Other-indicative', or as signs (*āyāt*) which indicate their Divine origin. For Nursi, the truth of this Qur'anic claim is self-evident, and it is the only truth that man can choose, if he is honest to himself, and if he wishes for salvation. For, according to Nursi:

> Belief makes man into man; indeed, it makes man into a king. Since this is so, man's basic duty is belief and supplication. Unbelief makes man into an extremely impotent beast. (*The Words*, transl. Vahide, 323)

If, as Nursi claims, man's quest should be to see all things as 'Other-indicative', the result is a vision in which all things in the created realm are invested with sacrality, pointing as they do to the transcendent Sacred, or God; the Nursian 'theology of the Beautiful Names', in which all created beings are 'manifestations' of the Divine attributes serves to complement this. However, one does not find in Nursi the kind of treatment of the dialectic of the sacred that we find, for example, in Eliade. For Nursi, the 'profane' is in the eye of the beholder, and lacks any real existence. To see things through the telescope of *ma'nā-i ismī* is to see them as *mulk* alone: it is to impose on them meanings which are inherently false and based on an illusion. Existentially, the profane is simply another way of conceptualizing what for Nursi is *sharr*, or 'evil'; and evil, in Nursi's theodicy, is nothing more than the 'lack of good', with no external existence to talk of.

Nursi's explanation of *ma'nā-i ismī* also helps to throw light on the much contested term '*ḥayāt al-dunyā*'. Miscomprehension of the term – and its mistranslation into English as 'the worldly life' – may have given rise to the notion that Nursi's attitude to material existence is a world-denying one. What Nursi rejects, however, is not the world per se, but the *ismī* attitude which bestows on created beings what amounts to virtually 'a life of their own' – hence the word *ḥayāt* – and an existence that is celebrated without any reference to the Divine. For Nursi, the world has three faces:

One is the mirror to Almighty God's Names, another looks to the hereafter and is its arable field, and the third looks to transience and non-existence. (*The Words*, transl. Vahide, 355)

This third face represents the world of those who 'worship the world', Nursi asserts, and who invest it with self-referential meanings alone, thus turning it into 'the source of all wrongs and the spring of calamities' (*The Words*, transl. Vahide, 356).

However, Nursi's notion of the 'self-referential' and the 'Other-indicative' has equal resonance for *homo religiosus* when applied to the behavioural domain, particularly in the context of 'practice' or 'righteous deeds'. For in the Nursian vision, what is true of the material constituents of the cosmos is also true of human behaviours, and particularly true of acts of worship. In fact, while Nursi does seem to preserve the notion of formal acts of worship, he asserts that all actions – so long as they do not contravene the sacred law – are worthy of being termed worship so long as the intention which fuels them is pure and Other-oriented:

Intention is a mysterious elixir changing ordinary acts and customs into acts of worship. (Nursi, *Epitomes of Light*, 132)

An action – any action – is thus considered sacred if it is connected directly to God and carried out in His name, and becomes profane only when that connection is broken or ignored. Nursi, like his coeval Eliade, thus avoids the dichotomy of 'the religious' versus 'the secular' by positing a world in which all things and behaviours are able to partake of sacrality so long as they are approached from the perspective of the 'Other-indicative' rather than the 'self-referential'. As a result, sacredness and profanity become states of mind rather than states of existence.

(iv) Nursi and causality

The issue of causality, or, more precisely, the necessity and efficacy of the causal nexus, is a long and vigorously contested problematic in the history of Muslim theological and philosophical debate. When fire touches paper, and paper ignites, is the fire the cause of the ignition, or is the effect – namely the flames which consume the paper – produced directly by God?[3] The Ash'ari theologians (*mutakallimūn*) were arguably the first to deny the existence of a necessary connection between cause and effect independently of God, who, as *musabbib al-asbāb*, they alleged, creates the effect directly. Centuries later, Ghazali championed the Ash'ari cause in his anti-Peripatetic tract, *Tahāfut al-falāsifa*. There, predating David Hume by several centuries, but for very different reasons, Ghazali theorized that the causal nexus to which we are all inured is only apparent: a human construct born out of the habit we have of linking events which occur together, such as the striking of the match, the touching of the match to paper, the ignition of the paper and its subsequent destruction by fire. To claim that the fire is in reality the cause of the paper's being reduced to ashes constitutes, in Ghazali's view, a slur on divine omnipotence and sovereignty. If causes actually possess the potency and duration needed to bring an effect into being, the role of God

---

[3] The complexity of the issue is such that any attempt to summarize it in space as limited as this is bound to lead to over-simplification. For a good introduction to the classical debates on causality, see Majid Fakhry's seminal *Islamic Occasionalism* (1958).

becomes virtually redundant: at best God then becomes a Prime Mover in the Peripatetics' sense of the term, with a nominal sovereignty akin to that of modern-day constitutional monarchs, who are kings of all they survey in name alone.

Nursi's repudiation of causality is informed by both the atomistic theology of the Ash'aris and the syncretism of Ghazali, whose disavowal of Peripatetic philosophy was articulated to a certain extent in their own language and on their terms. His motivation, too, was something that he shared with his ideological predecessor. Unlike the Ash'aris, whose sole objective seems to have been their desire to save divine sovereignty from the onslaught of the philosophers, Ghazali was fuelled in all of his endeavours – including his debunking of the Peripatetics – by an avowed intention to revivify belief among the Muslim masses. Eight centuries later, Nursi was moved to echo Ghazali's teachings on causality for almost identical reasons. However, the goalposts had now changed, and the old *bête noire* of Peripatetic philosophy had been joined by what Nursi claimed was one of its ideological offspring, scientific materialism. Founded on the premise of causal efficacy, scientific materialism was considered by Nursi to be the major threat to Muslim faith at the outset of the twentieth century. His rejection of the claims of scientific materialism runs through much of the *Risale* like a leitmotif, but finds its most trenchant expression in his treatise on nature and the causal nexus, *Tabiyat Risalesi*.

Nursi's treatise on nature rests on his refutation of a series of propositions which are, he says, 'commonly used and imply unbelief'. These include: the belief that causes create; the assertion that things form themselves; and the assumption that beings exist because 'nature' has created them. Furthermore, he adds, such propositions are put forward by believers, who fail to understand the implications of their own words (Nursi, *The Flashes Collection*, 233).

By invoking, *inter alia*, the cosmological argument, the anthropic principle, and the argument from design, and by employing the kind of dialectic championed by Ghazali in his refutation of the philosophers some seven centuries earlier, Nursi takes each proposition in turn and attempts to demonstrate what he considers to be the bankruptcy of these three central planks of naturalist – atheist belief in causality – his ultimate goal being to show that once reason has rejected these three, it has no option but to accept the fourth way: the way of Divine unity.

According to this fourth way, the created realm is one in which God's works are constant and continuous. Nursi says that God has two ways of creating: the first is through origination and invention, or *ibdā'*:

> That is, He brings a being into existence out of nothing, out of non-existence, and creates everything necessary for it, also out of nothing, and places those necessities in its hand. (Nursi, *The Staff of Moses*, 232)

The second way is through what Nursi terms 'composition' or *inshā'*:

> That is, He forms certain beings out of the elements of the universe in order to demonstrate subtle instances of wisdom, like displaying the perfections of His wisdom and the manifestations of many of His Names. Through the law of Providing, He sends particles and matter, which are dependent on His command, to these beings and employs the particles in them. (Nursi, *The Staff of Moses*, 232)

The creational modality known as *ibdā'* may be understood in the sense of instantaneous or *ex nihilo* creation, while *inshā'* may be termed 'developmental' in so far as it connotes growth and change *over time*. One is able to locate the Qur'anic antecedents for the Nursian schema of *ibdā'* and *inshā'* in verses such as 36. 82 – where the formula of *kun fa-yakūn* stands for *ibdā'* ('when He intends a thing, His Command is, "Be!", and it is') – and where verses such as 23. 78, indeed any verse which includes derivates of the verb *khalaqa* – stands for *inshā'*: 'It is He Who has created for you (the faculties of) hearing, sight, feeling and understanding...'

There is, however, a certain ambiguity in Nursi's reflections on these two kinds of creation. If, as he seems to imply, the modality of creation described as *ibdā'* corresponds to the *ex nihilo* creation suggested in several Qur'anic verses, his assertion that 'certain beings' are formed 'out of the elements of the universe' would appear to be at odds with this. While, it may be argued, the Qur'an is equally ambiguous on this score, there is nothing in its verses to suggest – as Nursi seems to do – that the two kinds of creation may be irreconcilable.

One possible solution would be to posit two modalities of creation working in tandem. On one level – the level of *inshā'* – each being is seen to be formed from other beings and developed over time: the nourishment and concomitant growth and evolution of the embryo in the womb *over time* is a salient example. On a more fundamental level, however, beings are created – and re-created – from instant to instant *ex nihilo*. On the level of *inshā'*, the creation of a being is analogous to the unfolding of a feature film: it is developmental, with one scene giving rise to the next in an unbroken causal sequence. On the level of *ibdā'*, however, each being is made up of a succession of instants that are causally unrelated, much like the individual frames of a film. Our perception of creation as the formation of beings from other beings persists partly because of our inherent inability, as creatures immersed in the space-time continuum, to discern the direct 'hand of God' which, the Qur'an asserts, creates all beings simply by commanding them to 'Be!'. In short, we see the moving film, and not the individual frames.

On the level of *mulk* or *shahāda* (the 'visible realm'), therefore, we see God's creative act in terms of a causal sequence; on the level of *malakūt*, or *ghayb* (the 'hidden realm'), God creates each effect directly, *ex nihilo*, and re-creates continuously, with nothing persisting for more than an instant.

The logical corollary of any disavowal of a truly efficient causal nexus can only be a form of occasionalism – be it Ash'ari, Ghazalian or Malebranchian – in which God creates and re-creates the world continuously from instant to instant. Unfortunately for us, while Nursi gives us many tantalizing glimpses of what may indeed amount to a kind of inchoate 'Nursian occasionalism', no such theory is ever articulated explicitly in the *Risale*. Whether one is excavated in the future depends on the skill and tenacity of those who take it upon themselves to dig down still further into Nursi's writings.

In short, then, Nursi's disavowal of causal efficacy brings creaturely focus back on God, who is seen not as one who created the world in six days and then rested on the seventh, but one whose creation and re-creation of the world is continuous and continual: were He for one second to withdraw from His creation, all would topple into oblivion. The enigma of the continuous effulgence of Divine light – however it is presented philosophically or theologically – serves to prevent man from attributing ownership to causes, and by extension to himself. Indeed, as the Nursian strictures on *anā* have shown earlier, the human predilection to attribute efficacy to causes stems from man's innate desire to claim ownership over everything he is and everything he does. The rejection of any necessary causal relationship between beings, implied by the notion of continuous creation, is also a rejection of the notion of human ownership of personal acts and attributes. Thus continuous creation strips man of all claims to godhood and returns the true ownership of all attributes of perfection to their rightful Owner.

(v) Nursi on belief (īmān) and submission (islām)

The fifth theme is Nursi's emphasis on the essential difference between belief (*īmān*) and submission (*islām*), and on their interdependence as a means for human salvation.

Implicit in the general Nursian discourse on Islamic orthopraxy is the notion that external submission to the will of God is predicable only on the possession of true, sustained and constantly reaffirmed belief, and that the 'externalia' of Islam – the practice of prayer, fasting and the like – are devoid of meaning without it. Belief in turn must be based on investigation and introspection, on deliberation and contemplation: without knowledge, belief cannot obtain, and without belief, submission is of little value.

In contrast to certain classical scholars who argued that belief is static, Nursi is one with the Hanafi theologians in his assertion that belief is subject to increase or decrease. Again, as with much of his general discourse, Nursi's writings on the subject are didactic and quasi-sermonical rather than academically theological: he writes not to prove some arcane point of *kalām*, but to guide and instruct:

> Since man himself and the world in which he lives are being continuously renewed, he needs constantly to renew his belief. For in reality each individual human being consists of many individuals. He may be considered as a different individual to the number of years of his life, or rather to the number of the days or even the hours of his life. For, since a single individual is subject to time, he is like a model and each passing day clothes him in the form of another individual. (Nursi, *Letters 1928–1932*, 391)

Belief in turn should, in the Nursian schema, lead to submission – *īmān* precedes *islām* – but not every believer in God will necessarily express submission to God's will in the form of adherence to the practical dictates of the *sharī'a*. Nursi describes such an individual as *gayrı müslim bir mümin*, or one who affirms intellectually the fundamentals of belief, such as divine unity, prophethood and the existence of the Last Day, but who falls short of implementing the 'pillars of Islam' (Nursi, *Risale-i Nur Külliyatı*, i. 360). By the same token, not everyone who claims to adhere to Islam is necessarily a believer. In verses such as those which outline the opportunism of the Banu Asad, the Qur'an (49. 14) uncovers the possibility of external submission without inner conviction: 'The desert Arabs say: "We believe." Say: "You have no faith; rather say: "We have submitted our wills to God", for faith has not yet entered your hearts. But if you obey God and His Messenger, He will not belittle aught of your deeds: for God is Oft-Forgiving, Most Merciful.' This means that while one is encouraged to assume that 'deeds of righteousness' – the indicator *par excellence* of external submission – are concomitants of belief, they are not necessarily so. In reality, 'deeds of righteousness' are in and of themselves no guaranteed indication of belief, as the response to the Banu Asad shows. Nursi's *dinsiz bir Müslüman* or 'unbelieving Muslim' presumably fits this bill.

Similarly, there are two modalities of submission – the formal and the internal, or upper case-I Islam and lower case-i *islām*, with the concomitant possibility, firstly, that some Muslims are not actually *muslim* in the Qur'anic sense of the word; and, secondly, that non-Muslims may also be considered *muslim*. While this more nuanced approach to the belief–submission issue is as far as we can discern absent from the *Risale*, Nursi was clearly aware of the difference.

Nursi is also clear on the need for both components – belief and submission – to be present as criteria for salvation: 'Just as Islam without belief cannot be the means of salvation, neither can belief without Islam be the means of salvation'. That belief should exist without external submission is anathema to Nursi, for 'Islam is taking the part of the truth and is submission and obedience to it' (*Letters 1928–1932*, 53). Similarly, Nursi fulminates against those who follow blindly, advocating at all times 'belief through investigation' (*tahkikî iman*) rather than 'belief through emulation' (*taklidî iman*; *Risale-i Nur Külliyatı*, 1511–12, 1721). Both states – belief without submission and submission without belief – are seen by Nursi as inherently self-defeating, leading ultimately to the ossification and gradual disappearance of belief.

While Nursi's teachings on belief and submission are significant on a purely religious level, they also offer important insights into the socio-cultural development of Muslim society as a whole, particularly in the context of the development of Muslim scholarship. For as I have attempted to show elsewhere, the *īmān–islām* issue not only renders explicable the bifurcation of the so-called 'religious sciences' into the 'rational' (*'aqlī*) and the 'scriptural' (*naqlī*), but it also helps to explain why the *faqīh* or jurist was able to attain such a high profile in the Muslim world of learning, and why the pursuit of jurisprudence came to be more prized than any other academic endeavour.

Furthermore, it provides a theoretical framework in which the phenomenon of nomocentrism – the expression *par excellence* of Muslim religious externalism – can be analysed and understood. Ghazali was the first scholar of note to bemoan the semantic shifts which had contrived to divest words such as *fiqh* of their spiritual significance and turn them into designations for *farḍ al-kifāya* sciences that pander to the ego of the practitioner on the one hand and to the religious exter-nalism of the masses on the other; Mulla Sadra was another. Nursi's elucidation of the *īmān/islām* dichotomy is a contem-porary variation of this age-old theme.

(vi) Nursi and the 'closed doors of creation'

The sixth theme comes in the form of a simple sentence which appears in *Ene Risalesi*, embodying an assertion which informs the whole Nursian endeavour, and in which can be found the subtext for the author's interpretation of the 'divine book' that is the cosmos, as well as the exegesis of the Qur'an by which that interpretation is paralleled. The assertion is made in an almost throwaway manner, and given the weight of the conceptual material on *ene* (*anā*) in which it is embedded, it is quite easily overlooked. The key to understanding the world, Nursi says, is in the hand of man, and is attached to the enigmatic *anā*, which is a yardstick enabling him to grasp the measure of all things, including the names and attributes of God. This is a key that man must use, Nursi asserts, for 'while being apparently open, the doors of the universe are in fact closed' (*kâinat kapıları zâhiren açık görünürken, hakikaten kapalıdır*: *Risale-i Nur Külliyatı*, 241).

For Nursi, the myth of the 'open doors of creation' is one of the biggest obstacles to human felicity, simply because it appears to demystify the world through the provision of spurious answers to the fundamental questions which man poses of himself and his surroundings while attempting to come to terms with the basic existential dilemma of his own being. Underpinning the 'open doors' paradigm is the assertion that the lion's share of man's most searching existential questions (Where am I from? Where am I now? What must I do? Where am I going?) have been answered in one way or other, and that those questions which remain unsolved will, one day, yield to human knowledge and achieve closure. Key to this future achievement are arguably what must seem, for Bediüzzaman, to have been two of the Enlightenment's most obdurately assertive and recalcitrant offspring: materialist – and, particularly, Freudian – psychoanalysis, which places man as the centre of his own universe, in obvious contra-distinction to the Nursian view of *anā* outlined above; and scientism, which bestows absolute epistemological primacy upon science, advocating the application of scientific theory and methods in all fields of enquiry about the world, including areas – such as morality, art, ethics and religion – which, its detractors claim, are outside its remit.

At the heart of scientism, of course, lies the acceptance on purely *a priori* grounds of the necessity of the causal nexus and the ubiquitous yet ethereal 'laws of nature', an ideological position which appears to repudiate all attempts to define the universe in any but the most mundane and material of terms. For the scientistically-minded scientist, the efficacy of causes and the primacy of 'natural processes' are taken as givens, and all subsequent discourse is mediated by those unquestioned assumptions. Attempts to bring God into the equation in any serious discussion with advocates of this approach is hampered from the outset by the uncontested premises upon which materialist science is founded. This, as the passage cited below shows, and as Nursi presumably would agree, would appear not only to close the door to future discussion, but to double-bolt it as well:

The first thing we must do in order to discuss the matter at all, of course, is to contrast the hypothesis of a creator with others supposedly competing with it. In thinking about this, we at once encounter two problems. First, *the events we usually call instances of 'creation' are themselves natural processes*, and this makes it a little difficult to get the intended contrast off the ground. Mary baking pies is a creative process, of a minor but nice sort; we don't think any magic is involved there. The pie grows *by purely natural processes*… (Narveson, 'God by Design', 90; italics added)

Implicit in this positivist paradigm, of course, is the notion that the material world is the only world that we can really comprehend *in and of itself*, and that man merely wastes his time thinking that anything mysterious, esoteric or otherworldly is at play in the universe. The concept of 'disenchantment' – the *Entzauberung* discussed by Weber[4] – can be traced back to the Romantic movement, where it was considered to be an unwanted and unnecessary effect of scientific progress. For Nursi, it is not scientific progress *per se* that is to blame for the tendency to see the doors of the universe as open, but rather the hubris which attends a scientistic approach to such progress. He himself advocates a form of 're-enchantment through revelation' which involves seeing past superficialities and acknowledging the Ground from which all things spring:

Know, O friend. Most of the knowledge of people about the earth and what they see as evident are based on a superficial familiarity, which is a veil spread on compound ignorance. They do not have any real foundations. For this reason, the Qur'an draws the attention of man to the usual and the ordinary. With its piercing expressions it draws aside the veil of superficial familiarity, shows man how things seen as usual and ordinary under the veil of familiarity are in fact extraordinary. (Nursi, *Epitomes of Light*, 323)

---

4 '*Entzauberung* refers mainly to the "contents" aspects of culture and describes the demystification of the conception of the world connected with growing secularism, with the rise of science, and with growing routinization of education and culture': S. N. Eisenstadt, 'Introduction', in: Max Weber, *On Charisma and Institution Building* (Chicago and London: The University of Chicago Press, 1968), p. li.

For Nursi, the 'open doors' paradigm is both a cause and a consequence of the apparent triumph of the *ismī* approach to the cosmic narrative over the *ḥarfī*, and can be combated only in the light of revelation and belief. For in Nursi's view, it is only by reading the cosmic narrative according to the epistemological precepts outlined by the 'line of prophethood' that man, desensitized by the claims of the 'line of philosophy', may regain his birthright and attain salvation through belief.

However, the myth of the open doors of creation is germane not only to Nursi's repudiation of causality and avowal of continuous creation, as discussed earlier. In the domain of disciplines such as jurisprudence, theology and exegesis, to claim that the teachings of any individual represent the last word on a particular subject is to lay the same kind of obstacles before the enquiring minds of men as the champions of scientism. Nursi's stance becomes clear in the occasional jeremiad levelled at certain iconic figures from the history of Muslim philosophy, whose elevated status in the collective memory of the Muslim *umma* tends, for Nursi at least, to conceal the fact that they are not all that they seem. Speaking of the predilection of certain renowned Muslim philosophers for the 'line of philosophy' and their implicit affirmation of the primacy of reason over revelation, Nursi berates them in no uncertain terms:

> It is because of these rotten foundations and disastrous results of philosophy that geniuses from among the Muslim philosophers like Ibn-i Sina and Farabi were charmed by its apparent glitter and were deceived into taking this way, and thus attained only the rank of an ordinary believer. *Ḥujjat al-Islām* al-Ghazzali did not accord them that rank even. (*The Words*, transl. Vahide, 565)

While Nursi's apparent disdain for philosophers such as Ibn Sina, Farabi and their Peripatetic peers is evidence not of any personal malice towards these individuals, but rather of his visceral approach to the question of authenticity, it can also be seen as a confirmation of his belief that no scholar or thinker can ever be said to have a monopoly on the truth. More importantly, his refusal to take on board the teachings of the 'great and the good' merely on account of their reputation in the eyes of the Muslim masses reveals an intellectual iconoclasm as refreshing as it is rare. Nursi wrote that if anyone were to ask him why he thought he could challenge such famous philosophers in this way, he would say:

> While having a pre-eternal teacher like the Qur'an, in matters concerning truth and the knowledge of God, I do not have to attach as much value as that of a fly's wing to those eagles, who are the students of misguided philosophy and deluded intellect. However inferior I am to them, their teacher is a thousand times more inferior than mine. With the help of my teacher, whatever caused them to become submerged did not so much as dampen my toes. An insignificant private who acts in accordance with the laws and commands of a great king is able to achieve more than a great field marshal of an insignificant king. (*The Words*, transl. Vahide, 568)

For Nursi, the truth is where it lies, regardless of whose hands it lies in. And to locate the truth only in the hands of those whose iconic status overshadows their actual claim to authenticity is to consider those 'doors of creation' to be closed, and all matters dealt with and understood. This is why the issue of orthodoxy in Islam is such a vexed and contentious affair: as soon as one fixes in intellectual aspic the contents and confines of orthodoxy, one proclaims that the 'ink has dried' on the issue, and all other bets are off. By following the example of Ghazali and exposing the erstwhile stars in the Muslim philosophical firmament as less than their champions claim them to be, Nursi remains true to his own strictures on the 'closed doors of creation', leaving room for the human intellect to explore the possibilities and, guided ultimately by the criterion provided by Divine revelation, discern the truth in a manner commensurate with its own capacities and potentialities.

4

Nursi on culture, society and politics

SUFISM

During Nursi's lifelong search for answers to man's existential dilemma, Sufism was one of the possible solutions he examined, and during his formative years he was influenced considerably by the writings of Jilani, Ghazali and Sirhindi. Indeed, he often described them as his 'spiritual poles'.

At the beginning of the 1920s, Nursi was seeking relief from his spiritual crisis and was forced to withdraw from society and seek out a safe haven far removed from Istanbul life. Gradually, as the 'Old Said' proceeded more in the rational and philosophical sciences, he started to look for a way to the essence of reality, as the Sufis (*ehl-i tarikat*) and the mystics (*ehl-i hakikat*) before him had done. To this end he retreated to Yuşa Tepesi, a hill on the Asian side of the Bosphorus near its junction with the Black Sea. The first source from which Nursi sought help was Jilani's *Futūḥ al-Ghayb*. On opening that book he came across the following line: *Anta fī dār al-ḥikma fa aṭlub ṭabība yudāwī qalbak*. His interpretation of this was as follows:

Oh, you unfortunate wretch! As a member of the *Darü'l-Hikmeti'l-İslâmiye*, you are like a doctor trying to cure the spiritual sicknesses of Muslims, whereas it is you who are sicker than all of them! You must first find a doctor for yourself before trying to cure anyone else! (Vahide, *Intellectual Biography*, 166)

Jilani's advice was appreciated, but for Nursi it was not enough, and so he continued his search. The second source, and an important catalyst in the transformation of the 'Old Said' into the 'New Said', was the *Mektûbat* of Shaykh Aḥmad Sirhindī. Nursi came across two letters in this book which appeared to address him directly, telling him to 'Make your *qibla* [the direction of your prayer, striving] one'. But Vahide (*Intellectual Biography*, 166–7) asserts that not even Sirhindi could give Nursi what he wanted. Indeed, none of the illustrious figures of Muslim mysticism, including greats such as Ghazali and Rumi, was able to fulfil his needs, and Nursi decided eventually that his only true 'master' was the Qur'an:

The head of these various ways and the source of these streams and the sun of these planets is the All-Wise Qur'an; the true single *qibla* is to be found in it. In which case, it is also the most elevated guide and most Holy Master. So I clasped it with both hands and clung on to it. (Vahide, *Intellectual Biography*, 167)

It is clear from Nursi's own words that, given the sociocultural context of his society, the way of the Sufis was difficult to follow and, as a method of reaching the truth, slow to produce results. He concluded (*The Letters*, 40) that the twentieth century was not the time for Sufism.

Nevertheless, the influence of mysticism on Nursi during his early career cannot be overstated, as evidenced by his subsequent writings. The wisdom of the mystics imbues his work, informs the metaphors that dot his language and finds expression in his approach to personal acts of devotion. He once said, for example, that he had recited over a period of fifteen days a collection of invocations taken from the writings of Sufis and mystics that usually take several months to recite. Furthermore, the *Risale-i Nur* lays great emphasis on contemplation of the cosmos and the 'signs of God' showcased therein – again, something that Nursi had in common with the Sufi sages. Nursi mentions a number of mystics and Sufis by name and acknowledges his debt to them. These include Ghazali, Shah Naqshband, Ahmad Sirhindi and Mevlana Khalid; interestingly enough, he also cites members of the household of the Prophet, such as 'Ali b. Abi Talib and his sons, Hasan and Husayn, and great Sufi 'poles' such as Junayd al-Baghdadi, as models for people to follow (Ashrati Sulayman, 'Nursi and the Qur'an', 82).

That Nursi received his early education from a number of prominent Sufi shaykhs of Eastern Anatolia has led some to speculate whether Nursi himself is to be counted among Sufi adepts. Such speculation would appear to be strengthened by Nursi's numerous references to Jilani, the founder of the Qadiri *tarikat*; Sirhindi (known as Imam-i Rabbani in Turkey), the founder of Muceddidi or 'Revivalist' Order; and Mevlana Khalid (1776–1827), the successor of the Muceddidi tradition and the link, it is claimed, between Sirhindi and modern Naqshbandi activism. According to Şerif Mardin (*Religion and Social Change*, 60), Nursi insisted that he was not only a Naqshbandi but also a Qadiri, and that his frequent references to Sirhindi lead one to think that by skipping lightly over the Khalidi link in his spiritual ancestry, he was trying to justify the novelty and distinguishing characteristics of his own movement. Evidence of this appeared early on in his career, when Nursi daringly chose as his spiritual mentor the founder of the Qadiri Order, rivals of the Naqshbandiyya. Mardin writes:

In a region where the Nakşibendi had established control by ousting the Kadiri this was a real act of defiance... One of the recurring themes in his later writing (and one which shows his universalism particularly well) is that one should have no special allegiance to any of the orders since all have something to contribute to Islam. (Mardin, 'Shaping of a Vocation', 72).

According to Algar, however, Nursi's formal allegiance to Sufism is not clear-cut:

Although he never submitted formally to the guidance of any *shaykh*, and regarded the structure and concern of the *tarikat* as inappropriate to the circumstances of the age, the influence of Sufism upon him was profound and can be seen to have permeated the entirety of his writings. (Algar, 'Nursi and the *Risale-i Nur*', 315)

Furthermore, Mardin suggests that despite the influence of Sufism on Nursi, his approach to the 'Sufi way', particularly later on in his life, was unequivocal:

Even though Said was educated in the tradition of the mystic orders he assumed an antagonistic stance towards them because he believed that re-instilling faith in the hearts of Muslims was more important than subtle arguments about the ways in which the divine showed itself. Nevertheless, his understanding and especially his interpretation of the Qur'an is marked by the mystic style. (Mardin, *Religion and Social Change*, 176)

As Mardin shows, Nursi's approach to the Sufi Orders reflects his criticism of those who overemphasize the importance of Sufism at the expense of serving the cause of spreading the truths of belief. Nursi discusses three categories of 'sainthood', claiming that the most excellent of these at this time entails following the practices of the Prophet and serving the truths of belief directly (*The Letters 1997*, 40). Included in this category, Nursi asserts, is the way to truth enshrined in the *Risale-i Nur*. In support of this assertion, he quotes Sirhindi, who wrote in his *Mektûbat*:

I prefer the unfolding of a single matter of the truths of belief to thousands of illuminations, ecstasies, and instances of wonder-working. (Nursi, *The Letters*, 40)

On the importance of the *Risale-i Nur*, and in response to those who dismiss it as the manifesto of a Sufi order, Nursi writes:

Since the reality of the matter is thus, my conjecture is that if persons like Shaykh ‘Abd al-Qadir Jilani (may God be pleased with him) and Shah Naqshband (may God be pleased with him) and Imam-i Rabbani (may God be pleased with him) were alive at the present time, they would expend all their efforts in strengthening the truths of belief and tenets of Islam. For they are the means to eternal happiness. If there is deficiency in them, it results in eternal misery. A person without belief may not enter Paradise, but very many have gone to Paradise without Sufism. Man cannot live without bread, but he can live without fruit. Sufism is the fruit; the truths of Islam, basic sustenance. In former times, through spiritual journeying from forty days to as much as forty years, a person might rise to some of the truths of belief. But now, if through Almighty God's mercy there is a way to rise to those truths in forty minutes, it surely is not sensible to remain indifferent to it. (*The Letters 1997*, 41)

According to Nursi, the purpose of all of the Sufi ‘ways’ is to expound the truths of belief. However, he avers, in the modern world it is difficult to reach the truth through the kind of spiritual purification advocated by classical Sufism. In the old days, most people believed in God and thus their only need was to perfect their belief, which, according to tradition, is capable of increase or decrease. The spiritual and individual life of the Sufis served Islam during these times and helped many to strengthen their faith in God. With the advent of modernity, however, and the rise of materialsm and atheism, many people have either lost or are in search of faith, and the only method appropriate today is one which appeals to both the heart *and* the intellect.[1]

Nevertheless, despite his criticism of Sufism, Nursi never actively opposed it. Indeed, he even attempted to legitimize it at a time when Sufi institutions and orders were proscribed by the political authority. In one of his letters, he writes that sainthood is a proof of prophethood, and the Sufi way a proof of the *shari'a*, and that both are a means of happiness.

> The aim and goal of the Sufi path is knowledge of God and the unfolding of the truths of belief through a spiritual journeying with the feet of the heart under the shadow of the Ascension of Muhammad (PBUH), to manifest the truths of belief and the Qur'an through illumination and certain states, and to a degree by 'witnessing'; it is an elevated human mystery and human perfection which is called 'the Sufi path' or 'Sufism'. (*The Letters 1997*, 518)

In short, Nursi himself was not a Sufi in the traditional sense of the word, and the movement he founded cannot be considered a Sufi order. Nevertheless, the influence of Sufism on his writings is such that one may be justified in calling him a 'non-Order-affiliated Sufi.' According to Mardin ('Shaping of a Vocation', 66), Nursi first appears as an aspirant Naqshbandi savant, and then as a Muslim ideologist. The *Risale-i Nur* movement is not a Sufi order, but a new kind of movement which, despite all the affection Nursi had for Sufism, could be included in the category of faith-based text movements.

But if Nursi is not a Sufi and the *Risale-i Nur* not a work of Sufism, and if the classical 'ways' of the Sufi adepts are inappropriate for modern man, exactly what is the nature of the spirituality to which, Nursi contends, man ought to aspire?

---

[1] According to al-Jilani, mystic intuition gives the recipient knowledge of reality that is not possible to gain through reason. See Dar, ' 'Abd al-Qadir Jilani and Shihab al-Din Suhrawardi,' 353.

The extent to which any discussion on spirituality can succeed – be it in the context of Islam in general, or Said Nursi's *Risale* in particular – depends on the degree to which the definitional opacity surrounding the term can be cleared. There are as many approaches to, and manifestations of, Islam as there are Muslims; the same applies to the notion of 'Islamic spirituality'. Definitions of 'spirituality' abound: as with the term 'mysticism', overuse has rendered it almost meaningless, particularly in Western secular milieus, where it is employed to denote anything and everything – from the contemplative traditions of Catholicism to the vague feelings of 'religiosity' claimed by those who do not adhere to any institutionalized faith yet continue somehow to feel at one with a 'higher force'. However, while we need to steer clear of the more stereotypical conceptions of 'spirituality' – particularly those which, in the context of Islam at least, connote some kind of false division between the 'material' and the 'spiritual', or, more misleadingly still, between the 'worldly' and the 'religious' – discussion cannot take place in a vacuum. Arguably the most appropriate place to locate the basic premises upon which a workable definition of the 'spiritual' in Islam can be found is the Qur'an. If the word 'spiritual' means 'connected to or concerning the spirit', then the Islamic revelation makes it abundantly clear that the human spirit is an 'uncreated' entity, 'breathed' into man by God Himself. Man's spirit is thus the uncreated 'breath of the Compassionate' (*nafas al-raḥmān*) within him that connects him to the divine and transforms an otherwise transient material being into the 'vicegerent' (*khalīfa*) of God on earth, capable of rising above all other beings to take his rightful place in eternity as the 'highest of the high'. In the Qur'anic – and, by extension, the Nursian – scheme, spirituality involves man's quest to uncover the reflection of the divine within himself.

The creation of human beings took place, it is held, not merely that they should affirm the existence of a Creator and bow down to His laws through various rites and rituals: for Nursi, God is not merely a principle that is to be accepted, or a giver of laws who is to be obeyed. While the God of the Qur'an is infinite, absolute, theoretically unfathomable and ultimately unreachable in the very real sense of those terms, He can be understood through His creation and, more importantly, His reality can be gradually 'uncovered' by man, who is able to approach God and become ever more aware of what He is, simply by virtue of the fact that he is created in God's image, with the capability of communion with the Source of his own being. In the cosmology of the Qur'an, which is confirmed by the *Risale-i Nur*, man is the reflection whose purpose in life is to perceive and understand the Reflected, and by so doing solve the existential riddle of his own being.

Qur'anic – and, by extension, Nursian – spirituality is therefore not about becoming more God-like. In fact it would appear to be quite the reverse. It is about realizing that those attributes in man which appear to make him like a god belong in reality to another. The 'spiritual journey' of man towards God, then, is not about becoming more like Him; rather, it is about 'purifying' oneself of all possible claims to 'god-likeness' and making room for Him to reveal Himself through the medium of the spiritualized soul. It means not acting like Him, but acting in His name; it involves not being like Him, but manifesting or revealing Him.

Man has been created to open and unveil (the treasuries of Divine Names and Attributes), be a luminous sign (guiding to God), receive and reflect (divine manifestations), be a light-giving moon reflecting the Eternal Power, and be a mirror for the manifestations of the Eternal Beauty (Nursi, *Epitomes of Light*, 300). For 'manifestation' to be realized, one has to clear out the 'clutter of the self' – the imaginary ownership that man exercises over his own attributes – so that His 'image' may be reflected in the mirror of man's being. It is this 'handing back' or 'surrender' to God of man's imaginary ownership over his own self that forms the bedrock of Nursi's approach to the 'spiritual'.

NURSI ON NATIONHOOD AND NATIONALISM

According to Nursi, notions of what comprises nationhood are constantly changing and differ according to historical circumstance and perspective. For Nursi, the components that comprise nationhood are language, religion and shared allegiance to a territorial entity; at least two of these must be present before one can talk in terms of nationhood. Race, however, is not a component. Hüseyin Çelik argues ('Nursi and the Ideal of Islamic Unity', 25–54) that Nursi opposes the crystallization of nationhood around race and highlights Nursi's comments on the argument forwarded by Prince Sabahaddin Bey. 'If we have to have "nationalism",' Nursi wrote, 'then Islam is enough for us.' According to Çelik:

> Bediüzzaman used the words 'nation' (*millet*) and 'nationhood' (*milliyet*) in accordance with their Arabic meanings. As is well-known, the word '*millet*' was originally used to denote a religion and membership of it; today, the word '*Ummah*' is used in its place. (Çelik, 'Nursi and the Ideal of Islamic Unity', 26)

In Nursi's understanding, nationhood is akin to a body, the spirit of which is Islam and the intellect of which is the Qur'an and belief. As Bernard Lewis points out, 'The Western concept of the nation as a linguistic, racial and territorial entity was not unknown to the Islamic orient, but was never the primary basis of group identity'; rather, group identity was 'the brotherhood of faith within the religious community, reinforced by common dynastic allegiance' (Lewis, *Emergence of Modern Turkey*, 53–5).

During the first period of his life, Nursi was acutely aware of the absolute necessity of achieving Islamic unity. After the Second Constitutional Revolution, many ideological approaches were explored with a view to halting the decline and fragmentation of the Ottoman Empire. The best known of these were Ottomanism, pan-Islamic unity and Turkism. Ottomanism had been the official ideology of the Tanzimat period, but survived only briefly during the Second Constitutional Period; the ideas most widespread among intellectuals of that time were pan-Islamic Unity and Turkism, with the latter subsumed under the general notion of Westernization.

It was at this juncture that Nursi first made his voice heard ('Divan-ı Harb-i Örfi', *Risale-i Nur Kulliyatı*, 1922) on the matter of pan-Islamic unity, joining those of Ali Suavi, Namık Kemal, Tevfik Fikret, Hoca Tahsin Efendi, Jamal al-Din al-Afghani and Muhammad Abduh. All of these were controversial figures in the Islamic world, be it because of their ideas or their activism. Nursi's acceptance of these thinkers did not extend beyond their ideas on pan-Islamic unity. According to Çelik ('Nursi and the Ideal of Islamic Unity', 248–9): 'Although their ideas on various subjects may be thought to be extreme in one way or the other, they had embraced the ideal of Islamic unity wholeheartedly.' It is clear, then, that Nursi was following contemporary currents in order to secure Islamic unity relatively early on in his career.

Nursi put great emphasis throughout his life on the need to prevent the fragmentation of the Muslim world: 'For the strongest bond of Arab, Turk, Kurd, Albanian, Circassian and Laz, and their firmest nationhood is nothing other than Islam' (*The Damascus Sermon*, 83). His belief that Islamic brotherhood was key to the whole issue of Islamic resurgence was something that should be seen primarily as a Divine command rather than as a means to political ends (Çelik, 'Nursi and the Ideal of Islamic Unity', 311–21).

One of the obstacles to Muslim unity, Nursi observed, was the penchant among peoples of the East for aping the nations of the West. 'An elderly preacher does not don the costume of a tango-dancer; blind imitation very often makes a man into a laughing-stock' (*The Letters, 1997*, 382). In various treatises Nursi criticizes the Asian countries for their blind and wholly inappropriate imitation of Europe and its institutions to the detriment of Muslim unity. As a result, he believed, the peoples of the East were becoming characterless. It was not that Nursi rejected every idea or innovation produced by Europe; indeed, he was in favour of Europe's many democratic and humanistic institutions, including both constitutionalism and, in later life, republicanism. What he rejected was the unqualified adoption of Western ideals for their own sake, without thought for their deleterious impact on Muslim societies.

With regard to nationalism, Nursi believed that there were two kinds. 'Negative nationalism', he says, is inauspicious and harmful: it is nourished by devouring others, persists through hostility to others, causes enmity and chaos and is fully aware of the havoc it wreaks. 'Positive nationalism,' on the other hand, arises from man's inner need for social cohesion and is the cause of mutual assistance and solidarity: it bestows strength on those who espouse it and is a means for further strengthening Islamic brotherhood. To love fellow-members of one's group is necessary if brotherhood and unity are to be preserved, and remains positive so long as superiority over others is not claimed. For Nursi there was no place for the kind of 'negative nationalism' that deems one race or nation superior to another, or which holds race or nationhood to be more important than religion.

Nursi regarded negative nationalism as a form of societal egoism. Throughout his life, he always identified three main obstacles to human happiness: ignorance, poverty and conflict. Negative nationalism, Nursi believed, is one of the key causes of conflict between Muslims. The solution, he believed, was the melting down of nationalistic feeling and the uniting of all Muslims under the umbrella of Islam. Nursi believed that working towards Islamic brotherhood and unity was a religious obligation and one of the most important means of societal change. His idea is supported by his own interpretation of the Qur'anic verse (49. 13):

> O mankind! We created you from [a single pair of] a male and a female, and made you into nations and tribes, that you may know each other.

According to Nursi, this means that God is saying to man:

> I created you as peoples, nations, and tribes, so that you should know one another and the relations between you in social life, and assist one another; not so that you should regard each other as strangers, refusing to acknowledge one another, and nurturing hostility and enmity. (*The Letters 1997*, 379)

According to Nursi, being divided into groups and tribes should lead to mutual acquaintance and assistance rather than antipathy and mutual hostility. At every opportunity, he tried to show how harmful racism can be. He also strove to convince his immediate audience that since time immemorial, their country had been witness to numerous migrations and demographic upheavals, with many outsiders drawn to settle there. Thus to construct movements and ideologies on the basis of race was not only meaningless but positively injurious to the health of society. For, he maintained, just as people cannot appoint their parents, so too they cannot chose their race or skin colour.

Finally it is worth mentioning that in spite of all the allegations levelled against him as a Kurd, Nursi resisted the demands of Kurdish nationalists to join them in their quest for the establishment of a Kurdish state built on the remains of the Ottoman Empire. There are those who claim that he did in fact support the cause of Kurdish nationalism. However, according to Nereid, there is nothing in either his writings or actions to support such claims. As Ibrahim Abu-Rabi writes (*Islam at the Crossroads*, 62): 'Even when the Ottoman Empire was abolished, Nursi refused to overplay his Kurdish card. He saw himself, first and foremost, as a Muslim scholar...' For Nursi, nationalism of any kind was a secular political phenomenon which would break the Islamic bonds between Muslims. With this stance, contrary to most Western-educated intellectuals of his time, Nursi supported the idea of pan-Islamic unity, rather than Western notions of nationalism.

JIHAD

Debates about Huntington's alleged 'clash of civilizations', with frequent reference to the religious foundation of these civilizations, are now endemic. Not only do they often fuel intense academic controversy but they also play a prominent role in popular understanding of the contemporary world, both as conveyed by the mass media and communicated to the general populace in the statements of political leaders. The driving force underpinning the Huntingtonian thesis is the perceived incongruity between the political–religious aspirations of the Muslim world – crystallized in the epiphenomenon known as 'Islamism' – and the ideals of the secular liberal West. And, increasingly, at the heart of Western concerns with regard to the perceived threat of 'Islamism' is the highly contested notion of jihad.

Indeed, over the past twenty-five years, and particularly since the atrocities of 9/11, the word jihad has acquired an unprecedented ubiquity, and for many has come to define the overarching approach of militant Muslim groups to their relations with the rest of the world. Increasingly, 'jihad' and the newly made-up word 'jihadist' have come to be equated with 'terrorism' and 'terrorist'. This is to an extent understandable, given that certain Muslim splinter groups have carried out offensives against Western interests under the umbrella of jihad. Nevertheless, even in situations in which jihad is argued by Muslims to be the embodiment of a legitimate expression of resistance, the word jihad itself continues to be construed as terrorism by the USA and its allies. The corollary of this is that jihad and terrorism are often conflated, and the image of Islam is distorted into something which has terrorism at its core. To this monochrome image of jihad, two main responses emerge from the vast generality of Muslims, mirroring the classical stances espoused by medieval theologians and jurists: one, supported by the 'jihadists' themselves that justifies the pursuance of jihad as an offensive strategy; and another, held by a large number of Muslim apologists and their Western liberal supporters, which holds that jihad may be resorted to only as a defensive measure. Beyond these two positions, voices that describe jihad in more nuanced tones or propose definitions of jihad which appear at first glance to be completely at odds with the perceived 'orthodoxy' of mainstream Muslim scholarship, are rarely heard. Bediüzzaman Said Nursi is one such voice.

Arguably a common denominator among otherwise disparate Islamic/Islamist groups and leaders of the past fifty to one hundred years has been the tendency to favour the use of force to change 'religiously suspect' regimes in the Muslim world and bring about Islamic revolutions. It is precisely on this point where one sees a fundamental difference between Nursi and his contemporaries. For not only is Nursi distinguished by his staunch opposition to any kind of uprising or revolution in the name of Islam, but also by his aversion to politics in general and the politicization of Islam in particular. Nowhere is Nursi's ideological departure from the majority of his contemporaries delineated more sharply than on the highly contentious issue of jihad.

PEACE, PUBLIC ORDER AND SECURITY IN THE TEACHINGS OF NURSI

While his contemporaries were seeking revolutionary change in the face of aggressive regimes, including in later years the secular state founded by Atatürk, Bediüzzaman Said Nursi saw obedience to the law as preferable to the possibility of anarchy (Horkuc, 'Nursi's Ideal for Human Society', 281). Believing Islam to be the middle way, Nursi advocated moderation and counselled the eschewal of extremes, referring at all times to the Prophetic tradition which has it that 'Too much or too little of anything is not good: moderation is the middle way' (*The Flashes*, 43) .

One instance in which his particular approach to moderation was made manifest came in his defence of Ibn ʿArabi, whose concept of the 'unity of existence' or *waḥdat al-wujūd* has attracted the opprobrium of countless orthodox Muslim scholars down the ages, some of whom have gone so far as to brand the Andalusian thinker an unbeliever (*kāfir*) who is beyond the pale of Islam. For Nursi, however, the issue is not cut and dried.

> While [Ibn ʿArabi] himself was rightly-guided and acceptable, not all of his works can be taken as sources of guidance and instruction.

> However, he himself is free of misguidance. Often, a word that is uttered may appear to betoken unbelief, even though the one who uttered it is not an unbeliever. (Nursi, *The Flashes*, 371)

He goes on to quote Ibn ʿArabi, who was remarkably circumspect with regard to the suitability of his own works for certain audiences:

> Those who are not one of us and who do not know our station should not read our books, for they may be damaging for them.

Nursi's insistence on even-handedness in the critique of others is also clear from his treatment of both Farabi and Ibn Sina (Avicenna); while he criticized both philosophers on a number of counts, he defended them from charges of unbelief (*takfīr*) levelled at them by other scholars.

Nursi's approach to Sufism and his attempts to reach common understanding with the Shiʿa also reflect his moderate views. Although he readily expressed the opinion that some people attached too much importance to Sufism at the expense of serving the cause of spreading the truths of belief, his respect for certain Sufi teachings and his unequivocal acceptance of the Sufi notion of sainthood demonstrate his insistence on avoiding any kind of dogmatic extremism. It is possibly on account of this moderate approach that both Nursi and his followers have been criticized harshly by other Muslim scholars and groups in Turkey for being 'soft', 'quietist', and overly accommodating of the *status quo*. Indeed, one prominent Turkish historian has gone so far as to claim that from the outset of his career, Nursi was a government agent in the employ of the Ottoman intelligence services.

Through his writings, Nursi asserted that public order and security were the means most conducive to producing the kind of environment in which social change might be obtained. To this end, he cautioned his readers to avoid any sort of action or behaviour that would lead to social discord, feelings of partisanship or discrimination, or situations likely to lead to a breakdown in public order and security. In this regard, the role of the *Risale* is seen by its own author as key:

> The *Risale-i Nur* cannot be broken; when attacked it grows stronger. It never has been used against this nation and country, and is not being used against them, and cannot be used against them. (Dilek, '*Risale-i Nur*'s Method and Aim', 129)

Nursi uses the term 'positive action' to describe what is needed in order to maintain social harmony and achieve the ultimate aim: the creation of a harmonious and healthy society through the renewal of personal faith. His political quietism is a direct reflection of this emphasis on the person: unlike some of his contemporaries, he never sought political power; nor did he condone any kind of movement designed to overthrow the state:

> Said Nursi, unlike Mawdudi, Qutb, or Banna, did not seek a political collective movement to control the state. He stressed the formation of an individual consciousness as a precondition for a just society. He wanted to offer a new conceptual ground to Muslims to defend their inner world against the expanding ideologies of the West. (Yavuz, 'Print-based Islamic Discourse and Modernity', 349)

According to Başar ('Positive Action', 148), for Nursi, maintaining public order is always positive, whereas fomenting conflict and differences, and disturbing public order and security, all constitute negative action. Similarly, to serve the cause of belief is positive, while to work for unbelief and immorality is negative; patience and thanks are positive, whereas impatience and rebellion are negative, and so on. Nursi was of the opinion that social calm and stability are a prerequisite for the implementation of the truths of the Qur'an in men's hearts and minds. In Nursi's understanding,

If events are considered not in the sequence 'reason–logic–reasoned thinking' but through the emotions 'excitement–physical force–partisanship' clashes become more violent and the social pulse races. (Dilek, 'The *Risale-i Nur*'s Method and Aim', 129)

In this regard it is important to point out that the last time Nursi met with his students before his death, he advised them explicitly concerning 'positive action'. He said:

Our duty is positive action, not negative action. It is purely to carry out the service to belief in accordance with Divine pleasure, and not to interfere in God's duty. We are charged to respond with thanks and patience to every difficulty within the positive service to belief, which preserves public order. (Cited in Dilek, 'The *Risale-i Nur*'s Method and Aim', 128)

Nursi considered the active prevention of any kind of unrest which may lead to anarchy to be the first step in establishing a just society, and there are a number of practical examples from his own life which reflect his concern with the preservation of order and harmony. However, it should be pointed out here that Nursi's quietism was not unconditional, and wherever he saw injustice, he would speak out against it, albeit using passive resistance. In his earlier years, for example, he opposed the aggressive and despotic policies of Sultan Abdülhamid II on the grounds that, in his opinion, these were in direct contravention of religious teachings. Later, despite having supported the Committee of Union and Progress in its formative years, he levelled strong criticisms against those members of the CUP who advocated violence as a means of realizing their political aims. And after the foundation of the Republic, he fulminated against the irreligious policies of the government, which, he believed, served to turn people not into secularists but into atheists. The contexts may have been different, but Nursi's opposition to anything deemed to contravene the laws and beliefs of Islam was a constant throughout. Nevertheless, though he criticized the materialist and irreligious policies of the republican governments with no uncertain vehemence, he never preached revolutionary activism as a means of preserving his Islamic ideals. Indeed, despite having written a highly controversial treatise in which, according to some commentators, Nursi identified Mustafa Kemal Atatürk as the *deccal (dajjāl)* or Antichrist, it should be pointed out here that throughout his life, be it in freedom, imprisonment or exile, he always prescribed positive action:

Nursi's life and teachings always preach non-violence and he asks his followers to pursue civic resistance. He derives this commitment to non-violence from the tenets of Islam and the Sufi perception of human dignity. Human dignity is the key and organizing principle of Nursi's writings. Although he invites Muslims to non-violence, Nursi examines the sociological background of violence. He identifies a number of conditions that impel people to resort to violence: ignorance, poverty and the lawlessness. Nursi argues that violence exists because power is not constrained and controlled by religious teachings. (Yavuz, 'Sufi Conception of Jihad: Said Nursi')

In short, the use of force within 'the realm of Islam' is, according to Nursi, impermissible; force may be used only against external aggression. Again, quoting Qur'anic verse 6. 164 – 'No bearer of burdens can bear the burden of another' – he states that at this particular juncture in human history there is a great difference between external jihad and internal jihad – an issue which we will deal with shortly. Action within the country, that is, within 'the sphere of Islam,' he believed, has to be 'positive action'. Since the destruction which threatens the Muslim community is not physical or material but rather moral and spiritual, *manevi* (*manʿawī*), the struggle against it has to be of the same kind:

Our duty is 'positive action,' not 'negative action.' It is solely to serve belief (in the truths of religion). [It must be] in accordance with divine pleasure, and not to interfere in God's concerns. [It is] the positive service to belief which results in the preservation of public order and security... (Vahide, 'Jihad in the Modern Age', 138)

At the centre of Nursi's concerns was the nurturing, maintenance and development of individual belief. For these to obtain, and for the relationship between man and God to be strengthened, public order and social harmony are not only useful and desirable; they are absolutely essential. For it is unbelief, according to Nursi, which disturbs public order and spoils it more than anything else. Nursi believed that he was trying to safeguard men from the threat of anarchy and encourage the establishment of social harmony through his *magnum opus*, the *Risale-i Nur*, which focuses first and foremost on the reform of the individual by emphasizing the constant need to renew one's belief in God. As an adjunct to this central theme of individual belief, Nursi posits five important principles which man must take on board if he is to avoid socio-political disharmony and unrest:

Five principles are necessary, nay, essential, at this strange time in order to save the social life of this nation from anarchy. These are: respect; compassion, refraining from what is prohibited (*haram*); security; and the giving up of lawlessness and being obedient to authority. (Nursi, *The Rays*, 372)

It is only through the implementation of these principles, Nursi avers, that the foundations of public order can be strengthened. The best evidence for this, he claims, is that in the space of no more than twenty years, the *Risale-i Nur* has transformed one hundred thousand people into peaceful and productive citizens.

Nursi's primary focus, then, is on the faith of the individual: the peace and security of the collective grows out of this, and cannot be imposed on society from above. The primacy of the individual is a recurring theme in many parts of the *Risale*. In this, Nursi mirrors the Qur'anic view, maintaining that an individual may not be sacrificed for the sake of a nation, and that certain rights enjoyed by society as a collective are not indispensable, particularly where the sanctity of an individual life is concerned.

The pure justice of the Qur'an does not allow the blood of an innocent individual to be spilt, even for the whole of humanity. For the two are the same, both from the point of view of Divine Power and the point of view of justice. But through self-interest man becomes such that he will destroy everything that forms an obstacle to his ambition: he will destroy the world if he can, and wipe out the whole of mankind. ('Seeds of Reality' in *The Letters 1997*, 549)

Other factors that contribute to social harmony, according to Nursi, are feelings of mutual tolerance, love, respect, and compassion – all of which must be nurtured carefully and kept alive if society is to thrive. For Nursi, these are the very feelings which make man human, and if they were to obtain in all societal institutions from family to state, then social tensions would be reduced to an absolute minimum.

What I am certain of from my own experience of social life and a whole life-time of study is this: the thing most worthy of love is love, and the thing most deserving of enmity is enmity. That is, love and loving, which render man's social life secure and lead to happiness, are most worthy of love and being loved. Enmity and hostility are ugly and damaging: they have overturned man's social life and more than anything deserve to be loathed and shunned... The time for enmity and hostility is over. Two world wars have shown how evil and destructive enmity can be, and what an awesome wrong it is. It has become clear that there is no benefit in it at all. (*The Damascus Sermon*, 49–50)

NURSI AND THE CONCEPT OF METAPHORICAL (*MAʿNAWĪ*) JIHAD

Nursi identifies two modalities of jihad: the internal and the external. Internal jihad concerns, *inter alia*, the sacrifice of the individual 'I' for the sake of the collective 'we' – a sacrifice necessitated by the conditions obtaining in the modern world, which lives in the age of the ego. Nursi believed that the present age demands from each individual a form of struggle with the soul known as *jihād al-akbar* (the greater jihad), for it is only the creation of a collective Islamic personality of this kind that can successfully contain the forces of misguidance and unbelief. It is worth noting, however, that nowhere in Nursi's *Risale* is explicit mention made of the saying attributed to the Prophet concerning the primacy of the 'greater' over the 'lesser' jihad.

Regarding external or physical jihad, Nursi's approach is something quite peculiar to him alone. While he accepts that, historically, the establishment, spread and progress of the rule of Islam occurred partly through the use of force, Nursi sees no place in the future of the Muslim community for military jihad. The use of weapons might have been justified in the past, Nursi admits, but as far as the future is concerned, it is the metaphorical swords of true civilization, material progress, truth and justice which will defeat and scatter the enemies of Islam.[2] In the Middle Ages, Nursi argues, Islam was compelled to respond to the hostility of its European enemies by resorting to warfare, yet in general managed to do so without forsaking its principles of justice

---

[2] In the original text he states: 'Kılıçlarınızı, fen ve sanat ve tesanüd-ü hikmet-i Kur'âniye cevherinden yapmalısınız.' See Bediüzzaman Said Nursi, "Divan-ı Harb-i Örfî," in *Risale-i Nur Külliyatı (The Epistle of Light)* (Istanbul: Nesil Basım Yayın, 1996), p. 1929.

and moderation: jihad was waged according to strict regulations, and Islam never instituted inquisitions or perpetrated genocide. In this regard, Nursi is of the view that force may be resorted to only to combat barbarity.

In today's world, however, Europeans are civilized and powerful; as a result, Nursi holds, the kind of hostility which existed in the medieval era no longer exists. As far as religion is concerned, Nursi says, the civilized can be conquered not through force but through peaceful persuasion: to this end, all that Muslims have to do is demonstrate the elevated nature of Islam with the 'tongue of mute eloquence' – namely by adhering to the precepts of Islam in their own lives and thus acting as ambassadors of Islam in the presence of others: 'Our action towards non-Muslims is persuasion, for we know them to be civilized, and to show them that Islam is [an] elevated [religion] and worthy of love' (Nursi, 'Divan-i Harb-i Örfi', 1930; see also *The Damascus Sermon*, 85). What remains problematic for modern readers of Nursi, however, is that he never defines exactly what he means by 'the civilized': throughout the *Risale*, the definitional boundaries of 'civilization' are never spelled out explicitly. For example, on several occasions he describes the Europeans as civilized yet never gives detail as to what the nature or foundations of their being civilized are. Defining Europeans as civilized without any elucidation of its meaning is arguably a result of the impact made on Nursi by the scientific and technological advances obtaining in the Western world during his lifetime. Despite this rather nebulous approach to the meaning of the term, Nursi's views on the means that Muslims are to employ in communicating their belief to others are unambiguous, as his own words show:

> Our way is concerned only with morality and religion... The way of our society is to love the love which Muslims feel for one another, and to loathe any enmity that may exist among them; its path is to be

moulded by the moral qualities of the Prophet Muhammad (PBUH) and to revive his practices (*sunna*); its guide is the illustrious *sharī'a*; its sword is decisive logical proofs; and its aim is to uphold the word of God... [Our] society's .... way is to wage the greater jihad (*jihād-i akbar*) with one's own [evil-commanding] soul, and to guide others. Ninety-nine percent of [its] aspiration is directed not to politics, but to licit aims that are the opposite of politics, such as the nurturing of fine morals, right conduct, and so on... (Vahide, 'Jihad in the Modern Age', 129)

His emphasis on moderation and passive resistance notwithstanding, it should be pointed out that when it came to the defence of his country, Nursi did not shrink from active participation. For example, at one point he became commander for a volunteer militia force and served at the front; he was later wounded, captured and taken to the province of Kostroma in north-western Russia as a prisoner of war. As Vahide points out ('Jihad in the Modern Age', 130), Nursi took part in a number of 'physical encounters' in defence of his country during the First World War. His military adventures aside, Nursi's view that the essential struggle in the modern age should be based on the furthering of science, progress, and civilization, together with the revival of the Prophet's *Sunna* and precepts of Islamic morality, was one that remained constant throughout. Nursi's jihad was always to enjoin the good and to counsel against evil, and to serve religion by calling others to believe in God. Nor was his focus directed solely at the fate of his Muslim co-religionists. As Michel states:

Writing during one of the most tragic periods in the history of Anatolia, Said Nursi could not ignore the reality of the deaths of so many innocent persons. It is to his great credit that he rose above sectarian loyalty to address the question of innocent Christians as well as Muslims who fell victim to the times. 'Even if those innocent people were unbelievers,' he stated, 'In return for the tribulations they suffered due to that worldly disaster, they have such a reward from the treasury of Divine mercy that if the veil of the Unseen were to open, a great manifestation of mercy would be apparent in relation to them and they would declare, "O Lord, thanks be to You! All praise belongs to God." ' (Thomas Michel, SJ, 'Muslim–Christian Dialogue and Cooperation', 330–1)

From the early 1920s to the very end of his life, Nursi's jihad consisted, according to Dilek ('The *Risale-i Nur*'s Method and Aim', 128), in educating people through his writings and in stressing the centrality of the concept of metaphorical (*ma'nawi*) jihad to the teachings of the *Risale-i Nur*. Thus the greater part of Nursi's endeavour was concerned with education and educational reform, at the heart of which lay his aspirations for a rapprochement between the religious and the modern sciences. Nursi was one of a handful of scholars in Turkey at that time who criticized Muslims themselves for their backwardness. He pointed out that the essential enemies of the Muslim world were ignorance, poverty and conflict – all of which he identified as contributory factors to the scientific and technological backwardness of the Muslim world in comparison with the West. The solution, he believed, lay in the taking up of weapons – but weapons of industry, learning and, above all, unity. It was these 'pitiless' enemies and their consequences, he thought, that had been the cause of the Islamic world's decline, and had served to prevent Muslims from performing the duty of upholding the word of God. As Nursi himself writes:

All believers are charged with upholding the word of God. At this time, the most effective means of doing this is through material progress, for the Europeans are crushing us under their 'immaterial' tyranny with the weapons of science and industry. We must therefore wage jihad with the same weapons against 'ignorance, poverty and the conflict of ideas,' the most fearsome enemies of upholding the Word of God...[and] from the point of view of religion, the civilized are to be conquered through persuasion, not by force, and by demonstrating through compliance with its precepts and by good morals, that Islam is elevated and worthy of being loved. (Vahide, 'Jihad in the Modern Age', 127)

Today, certain Muslim apologists are at pains to identify jihad with the kind of striving that is conducive to spiritual progress – the *jihād al-akbar* said by the Prophet to outshine in importance the *jihād al-aṣghar* – the physical fighting which the Qur'an refers to consistently as *qitāl*, all of this notwithstanding the dubiety of provenance which attends the ḥadīth in question.

Others admit freely that in earlier times, jihad was condonable not only as a defensive stratagem but also a means whereby non-Muslims were subdued. There appears to be, therefore, a range of opinions attending the issue of the nature and permissibility of the particular component of jihad known as *qitāl*. That there is a diversity of jurisprudential opinions on the issue attests to the ambiguity of the verses in question and their innate openness to contextual interpretation.

Historically the debate on jihad has always focused on whether it is defensive, offensive or both; or on the difference between the greater and the lesser jihad. Nursi turns this on its head by proscribing military jihad altogether, and saying that Islam is not to be defended by the sword – since it is no longer identifiable as a geographical as well as a religious entity – but by the force of reason, progress and civilization.

5

Conclusion

Bediüzzaman Said Nursi emerges from these pages as a modern thinker whose contribution to the dissemination of Qur'anic teachings in general, and the revival of belief in particular, is possibly without equal in the past 150 years. Born at a time when the external challenges to the Muslim world were many, and its internal problems both complex and apparently insurmountable, he made it his goal to reintroduce the teachings of the Qur'an to a generation for whom the truths and realities of Islam had fallen into desuetude. Realizing that, in order to do this, he must equip himself with all the tools and accoutrements of modern scholarship, he added a mastery of philosophy and the modern sciences to his already considerable expertise in the classical Muslim fields of theology and exegesis.

Nursi's engagement with the new scholarly disciplines of the twentieth century must, of course, be set in its historical context. The increase of Western and Westernizing influences in the decaying Ottoman Empire of the late nineteenth century, together with the rise of doctrines such as dialectical materialism, scientism, social Darwinism and Freudianism, and the concomitant attacks on religion in general, and on Islam in particular, were catalysts which galvanized Nursi into action and helped shape his life's mission: to spread the teachings of Islam not with the material sword of jihad, the militant expression of which, like all politics, he eschewed, but with the metaphorical sword of the Qur'an and its truths. It was the exposition of these truths, as the basis for the revival of belief, which occupied most of his adult life, culminating in one of the most remarkable feats of Muslim scholarship to emerge in the past five centuries, the magisterial *Risale-i Nur*.

The themes and concepts outlined in Chapter 2 ('Thought and Teachings') lie at the heart of the *Risale*, forming the pillars which support Said Nursi's teachings. That they are key to his perception of the spiritual is understood from the centrality of one or more of these concepts to every treatise in the complex of epistles known as the *Risale*. They are concepts which, when understood as a unity, offer a framework in which the Creator/created relationship can best be understood. And it is the decipherment and deconstruction of man's position vis-à-vis the Ground of his being that provides the opportunity for *communion*, which is the objective of all spiritual endeavour. Without Nursi's conception of the human 'I', for example, his exposition of the 'beautiful names of God' is little more than eloquent but ultimately meaningless gnostic theology, while without the repudiation of cause and effect, Nursi's teachings on the wiles and deceits of the human 'I' lose most if not all of their potency. In line with his rejection of the efficacy of causes is his affirmation of the 'Other-indicative' over the 'self-referential', thus completing his sacramental view of creation. Each pillar of thought lends credence to the other, and to Nursi's overarching spiritual edifice as a whole.

Each of the themes discussed in Chapter 2 represents a concept, notion or principle which Nursi deems essential for man in his quest for meaning, authenticity and salvation, and central to his attempt to solve man's most pressing existential dilemmas. They may not be concepts originated by Nursi himself, though it is tempting to consider them his by virtue of the innovative, eloquent and highly idiosyncratic way that he expresses them. Furthermore, they are concepts which, despite their importance, have not received the scholarly attention they warrant. While important work has now begun on the *Risale*, it is still almost completely virgin territory. Whether the concepts under scrutiny here are of crucial importance for every individual is a matter of personal belief and private conscience. On a purely academic level, however, they are concepts that researchers in the field of contemporary Muslim thought cannot afford to overlook. From the tenor of his writing, there can be little doubt that they are concepts that Nursi himself considered seminal – not only in the sense of their centrality to his own view of the world, but also as conceptual foundations for an authentic interpretation of the Islamic revelation and, consequently, a reading of the cosmic narrative which, as Nursi suggests, man has no option but to try to decipher. As such, unless these concepts are subjected to rigorous critical appraisal by philosophers, sociologists and psychologists of religion, as well as by theologians and scholars of Islamic gnosis, the surface of Nursi's work will remain barely scratched, and, in the West at least, Nursi's *Risale* will continue to be seen as little more than a fascinating yet poorly-understood curio.

In the contemporary Muslim world, however, especially in the Turkish-speaking part of it, Said Nursi's reputation as a thinker, communicator and renewer of religious belief is arguably without parallel. This is borne out by the existence of a faith-based movement, known as *Nurculuk*, which emerged gradually as Nursi's career developed. The name *Nurculuk* was given to the nascent community of followers by elements in the Turkish press, possibly with the intention of presenting the disciples of Nursi as some kind of brotherhood akin to a Sufi order or *ṭarīqa*. Nursi himself, however, was always at pains to eschew such connections. Rejecting the notion that his followers should form an organized body, let alone a brotherhood, Nursi referred to them simply as 'those who follow the Epistle of Light' (*Risale-i Nur talebesi*).

That an organized body – or, rather, confederation of loosely affiliated groups – did actually emerge after his death is perhaps inevitable, given the charisma of the man and his work. Dedicated to the promulgation, discussion and implementation of Nursi's teachings, the adherents of *Nurculuk* – or Nurcus, as they are most commonly known – today number in excess of an estimated seven million worldwide. The achievements of the various groups, both in Turkey and further afield, are considerable. At the grassroots level, Nurcu devotees meet at least twice a week in specially designated study circles, or *ders*, to discuss various aspects of Nursi's teachings as enshrined in his *magnum opus*, the *Risale-i Nur*; a recent survey estimated the number of such weekly circles in Turkey alone as more than five thousand, with several thousand more taking place across Europe and the United States. In Britain for example, wherever Turks – and Turkish students in particular – are found in any appreciable number, the existence of at least one weekly *ders* may be taken as given.

Since Nursi's death in 1960, the elders of the Nurcu movement – the *ağabeys* or 'brothers' – have worked hard to keep alive the legacy of their spiritual master. Nowhere is this more evident than in the efforts made to disseminate the teachings of Nursi in published form. While certain sections of the *Risale* appeared in print during Bediüzzaman's lifetime, the past twenty-five years have witnessed not only the publication of the complete works of Said Nursi in Turkish, but also the translation of most of the *Risale-i Nur* into different languages. The labour of publishers such as the Risale-i Nur Enstitüsü, Yeni Asya Neşriyat and Sözler Publications has been such that the writings of Said Nursi have been able to attain a readership unprecedented in his lifetime. To supplement the dissemination of Nursi's written works, newspapers, radio channels and a number of important educational and research institutions have also been set up in Turkey and abroad in order to present a worldview imbued with the spirit of Nursi's teachings. Of all of this, the biennial Said Nursi Symposium, held in Istanbul, is possibly the crowning achievement. Attracting scores of visiting scholars from all over the world, who present papers on all aspects of Nursi and his works before audiences counted in their thousands, the symposia and the books which emerge from them have become an important vehicle for the communication of Nursi's discourse to international academe. Since the first International Symposium in Istanbul in 1991, Bediüzzaman Said Nursi has gone from being a relatively unknown figure to almost a household name, and his reputation as a scholar of inestimable importance has grown commensurately. We hope that the present work, showcasing the highlights of Nursi's discourse, will enhance that reputation and encourage an even wider audience to seek knowledge and understanding of one of the modern Muslim world's most original thinkers.

6

Further reading

Life and works

The standard English language work of reference on the life and works of Bediüzzaman is Şükran Vahide's *Islam in Modern Turkey: An Intellectual Biography of Bediüzzaman Said Nursi* (2005), a revised version of her earlier biography, *The Author of the Risale-i Nur: Bediüzzaman Said Nursi* (2000). The leading translator of Nursi's works into English, Vahide traces Nursi's life and career from his birth in the Eastern provinces of Turkey in 1877 to his death in 1960, producing an engaging narrative from a remarkable synthesis of primary sources. Vahide's grasp of her subject is unmatched, and this work has all the hallmarks of a future classic in the field of scholarly biography.

For those able to access biographical material on Nursi in Turkish, the works of Necmeddin Şahiner, upon which we have drawn extensively in this study, should be the first port of call. His five-volume *Son Şahitler Bediüzzaman Said Nursi'yi Anlatıyor* (1980–1992) is a magisterial work, comprising a weighty body of recollections, anecdotes and memories distilled from hundreds of interviews conducted over a number of years with people who knew or who had met Bediüzzaman in the 'New Said' period of his life. Şahiner's biography of Nursi, *Bilinmeyen Taraflarıyla Bediüzzaman Said Nursi (Kronolojik Hayatı)* (1998), has gone through several editions in Turkey and is also a major source for those interested in Turkish language material on our subject.

While Nursi gives away little about himself in his writings, we can gain important insights into certain major events in his life from a number of his works. This is particularly so with regard to his political activities during the 'Old Said' period, tantalizing glimpses of which we are afforded from time to time in his works. One such example is the *Divan-ı Harb-ı Örfî*, the defence speech given by Nursi after the so-called '31st March incident', and which led to his acquittal. The *Divan-ı Harb-i Örfî* can be found in Bediüzzaman Said Nursi, *Risale-i Nur Kulliyatı* (1996), pp. 1918–35.

Similarly, Nursi's opinions on constitutionalism and the freedom movement can be gleaned from the question-and-answer sessions that comprise his *Muhâkemat* (Reasonings) and *Münâzarat* (Debates), both of which can also be found in the *Risale-i Nur Külliyatı*, at pp. 1984–2040 and 1938–60 respectively.

Another invaluable source of information on Nursi, the development of the *Risale-i Nur* and, in particular, the genesis of Nurculuk as a faith movement is Ali Mermer's *Aspects of Religious Identity: The Nurcu Movement in Turkey* (1985). The first academic work on the Nurcu phenomenon undertaken in the UK, this sociological study throws considerable light on organizational aspects of the movement and its evolution in Turkey during the two decades following Nursi's death.

Thought and teachings

The six main themes discussed in Chapter 2 are, of course, best understood through Nursi's own words, and so the interested reader is urged to read some of the key treatises which can be found in the four main books that make up the *Risale-i Nur.* A word of caution, however, is necessary here. While Şükran Vahide has excelled in her translation of Nursi's works, the *Risale* in English is not an easy read. To a certain extent, this is due to the fact that, in parts, the original is often abstruse and circumlocutory – a result, perhaps, of the fact that the Nursian idiolect is for the most part a bewildering amalgam of Ottoman Turkish, Persian and Arabic, woven together in seemingly endless sentences, which can often be quite taxing on even the most forbearing of readers. In remaining loyal to the original without compromising the meaning, Vahide's performance on this most slender of translational tightropes does not always come off, though the sincerity of intention and the integrity of her overall endeavour are irrefragable.

Its complexities notwithstanding, the English translation of the *Risale-i Nur* must be the first resort for those wishing to gain deeper insight into Said Nursi's thoughts and teachings. Our recommendations for further reading for this chapter cover each theme in turn, indicating first those texts from the *Risale* which are both appropriate and accessible, and then the secondary sources which supplement the topics covered by those texts.

On the primacy of belief in Nursi's discourse, a good introduction for the interested reader would be his 'Twenty-Third Word'. This looks at the virtues of religious belief and juxtaposes them with the demerits of unbelief and atheism: see Said Nursi, *The Words* (2002), pp. 319–27. A readable exposition of Nursi's approach to belief is Imtiyaz Yusuf,

'Bediüzzaman Said Nursi's Discourse on Belief in Allah: A Study of Texts from the Risale-i Nur Collection' in *The Muslim World (The Special Issue: Said Nursi and the Turkish Experience* (1999), pp. 336–50.

What has been called in this chapter Nursi's 'theology of names' is a leitmotif that runs through the whole of the *Risale-i Nur*, and choosing just one treatise or chapter which deals with this subject is both difficult and invidious. For a deeper understanding of how Nursi sees God's 'Most Beautiful Names' as the pillars upon which the cosmos is founded, arguably the best starting point is the 'Seventh Ray', also known as *The Supreme Sign* in Said Nursi, *The Rays* (2002), pp. 123–98. Chronicling the spiritual journey of a 'traveller questioning the universe concerning His maker', the *Supreme Sign* showcases the universe as a vast gallery of 'signs' waiting to be interpreted by man, and all of which, in their totality, point to the various names and attributes of God as He manifests Himself in creation. As such it is one of Nursi's most engaging and accessible treatises and a good general point of entry for anyone encountering the *Risale* for the first time.

On the centrality in Muslim spirituality of the 'divine names', readers versed in Arabic and Persian are directed to 'Abbas Qummi's *Mafātīḥ al-jinān* (n.d.). The *Mafātīḥ*, the most popular book of liturgy among the Shi'a, is a treasure-trove of invocations, supplications and meditations based on or around the 'Beautiful Names', including the famous *Jawshan al-kabīr*. The *Jawshan*, an invocation which involves recitation of a thousand divine names and attributes, and which is usually traced back to the Prophet through his great-grandson, Zayn al-'Abidin, is a clear source of inspiration and support for much of Nursi's 'theology of names'. He cites it frequently and its impact on him is evident in the tenor of his writing. For Nursi's own take on the importance of the *Jawshan*, see *Risale-i Nur Külliyatı*, vol. 2, pp. 1745–6.

Several English translations of the *Jawshan* exist, including one by Şükran Vahide, which can be found online at <www.rso.wmich.edu/mda/jawsan/index.htm>.

For a rather different but not totally dissimilar view of the hierophanic nature of creation, namely that of Nursi's coeval, Mircea Eliade, see Douglas Allen, *Myth and Religion in Mircea Eliade* (2002), pp. 74–83.

Said Nursi's discussion of the nature and function of the human 'I' or *anā* (*ene* in Turkish) appears in his penetrating *Ene Risalesi*, which forms the 'Thirtieth Word' of *The Words* pp. 557–69. One of his most thought-provoking treatises, the 'Thirtieth Word' is not the most accessible of texts, however, and readers may wish to supplement their study of the original with Colin Turner's attempt to simplify the text somewhat in his *Islam: the Basics* (2005), pp. 150–9.

For more on the Nursian antinomy of the *ismī* and the *ḥarfī*, or the notion of the 'self-referential' and the 'Other-indicative', Nursi's 'Twelfth Word' is as good a starting point as any. A comparison between 'the sacred wisdom of the All-Wise Qur'an and the wisdom of philosophy and science', this can be found in *The Words*, pp. 143–9. Interesting parallels may be drawn between Nursi's thesis and the notion of the sacred and the profane in Eliade's discourse. For this, see Douglas Allen, *Myth and Religion in Mircea Eliade*, pp. 65–99.

With regard to Said Nursi's disavowal of proximate causality, his *Tabiyat Risalesi* ('Treatise on Nature'), in which this notion is explored in great depth, can be found in its entirety in *The Flashes* (2004), pp. 232–54. For those wishing to explore other Muslim approaches to this hotly contested issue, causality according to the Ghazalian perspective is a relatively well-covered area of research, although articles are of vastly differing quality. One of the more accessible is: Stephen Riker, 'al-Ghazali on Necessary Causality', in *The Monist*, vol. 79, no. 3, pp. 315–24.

The distinction between belief (*īmān*) and submission (*islām*), and the imperative that belief follow from investigation (*taḥqīq*) rather than imitation (*taqlīd*), form another Nursian trope which underpins much of his discourse. While there is no treatise dedicated in its entirety to this subject, Turkish language readers may wish to consult Nursi's *Barla Lâhikası* in *Risale-i Nur Külliyatı* (1996), vol. 2, pp. 1511–12 and 1553–4. For an analytical survey of various theological and jurisprudential positions on this issue in classical Islam, see Colin Turner, *Islam without Allah? The Rise of Religious Externalism in Safavid Iran* (2000), pp. 1–20.

On the issue of the apparently 'closed doors' of creation and the challenge posed to religious belief by materialism, positivism and scientism, readers are referred once more to Nursi's *Tabiyat Risalesi*. The treatise on the human 'I', also mentioned above, is worth reading, for it is there that Nursi's strictures on the 'closed doors' of creation are contextualized. As for secondary sources, the question of scientism is briefly and efficiently dealt with by Michael Shermer in his 'The Shamans of Scientism' in *Scientific American*, June 2002, p. 35.

Finally, Nursi's views on *waḥdat al-wujūd* are well-documented and appear at various points throughout the *Risale*. See, for example, his 'Second Important Example' in the Eighteenth Letter of *Mektubat* (The Letters), published as Said Nursi, *The Letters 1928–1932* (1994), pp. 106–9. On the balance between *tanzīh* and *tashbīh* insofar as it pertains to Ibn 'Arabi's conception of *waḥdat al-wujūd*, see William C. Chittick, 'Ibn 'Arabi' in S. Hossein Nasr and Oliver Leaman (eds.), *History of Islamic Philosophy* (2001), pp. 501–3.

Culture, society and politics

While Nursi cannot be classed as a Sufi in the conventional sense of the word, the impact of various Sufi thinkers and their teachings on his work is undeniable. For further insight into some of these influences, readers may wish to consider a number of secondary sources which deal with the major figures referenced by Nursi in the *Risale*. On 'Abd al-Qadir al-Jilani, for example, see B. A. Dar, ' 'Abd al-Qadir Jilani and Shihab al-Din Suhrawardi', in M. M. Sharif (ed.), *A History of Muslim Philosophy* (1999), pp. 351–3. For the history of the Qadiri order and its impact in the late Ottoman era on the Eastern provinces of Anatolia, see M. van Bruinessen, *Agha, Shaikh and State: The Social and Political Structures of Kurdistan* (1992), pp. 216–21.

On the teachings of Shaykh Khalid-i Baghdadi, the most accessible secondary source is Albert Hourani, 'Shaikh Khalid and the Naqshbandi Order' in *Islamic Philosophy and the Classical Tradition* (1972), while a brief but enlightening introduction to the intellectual phenomenon that was Ibn 'Arabī can be found in A. E. Affifi's 'Ibn 'Arabi', in M. M. Sharif (ed.), *A History of Muslim Philosophy*, pp. 415–18.

For further insights into Nursi's approach to the twin issues of nationhood and nationalism, readers should consult Şükran Vahide, *Islam in Modern Turkey: An Intellectual Biography of Bediüzzaman Said Nursi* (2005), pp. 60–2 and 190–2. Said Nursi's views of race as a component of nationalism can be found in *The Letters* (1994), pp. 380–4. On the dangers of racialism and the issue of 'positive' as opposed to 'negative' nationalism, the 'Third Topic' of Nursi's 'Twenty-Sixth Letter' in the same *Letters* (pp. 379–85) is also worth reading.

On political involvement, public order and jihad, there are a number of primary and secondary sources to which readers may wish to refer:

Hasan Horkuc's 'Said Nursi's Ideal for Human Society: Moral and Social Reform in the Risale-i Nur' (2004) is a good starting-point for deeper insight into Nursi's take on a whole host of socio-political issues. On public order and the issue of tolerance and moderation, for example, see pp. 281–2; on the prevention of unrest and anarchy, see pp. 316–17. Horkuc deals with Nursi's aversion to militancy and his implicit rejection of the status quo on pp. 283–4, and with the notion of 'metaphorical jihad' on p. 289.

With regard to Nursi's tacit rejection of Kemalism, an interesting original source is his treatise on the 'Signs of the End of Time', in which, it has been claimed, Atatürk is identified as a possible candidate for the *dajjāl* or Antichrist. The treatise can be found in Nursi's *The Rays* (1998), pp. 97–114. Unsurprisingly, the writing of this treatise culminated in Nursi's arrest and trial, at which he was acquitted.

In 'New Muslim Discourses on Pluralism in the Post-modern Age: Nursi on Pluralism and Tolerance' (*The American Journal of Islamic Social Sciences*, 2002, pp. 80–1), Horkuc goes more deeply into the Nursian argument on moderation; John Voll covers similar ground in his 'Renewal and Reformation in the Mid-Twentieth Century: Bediüzzaman Said Nursi and Religion in the 1950s' in *The Muslim World* (1999), p. 254.

For Nursi's own exposition of tolerance and moderation, see *The Words* (1992), pp. 565–6 and *The Letters* (1997), p. 518. On unbelief as a force antithetical to the spirit of tolerance and moderation, and deleterious to the maintenance of social order, an accessible secondary source is Niyazi Berki, 'The Qur'an and its Method of Guidance' in *A Contemporary Approach Towards Understanding the Qur'an: the Example of the Risale-i Nur* (1998), pp. 96–9.

Finally, those readers who wish to explore Nursi's ideas on jihad, both actual and metaphorical, are referred in the first instance to Şükran Vahide's chapter titled 'Said Nursi's

Interpretation of Jihad' in Ibrahim Abu-Rabi (ed.), *Islam at the Crossroads: On the Life and Thought of Bediüzzaman Said Nursi* (2003), pp. 93–114.

Bibliography

Abu-Rabi, Ibrahim (ed.), *Islam at the Crossroads: On the Life and Thought of Bediüzzaman Said Nursi* (Albany: SUNY Press, 2003).

Affifi, A. E., 'Ibn ʿArabi' in M. M. Sharif (ed.), *A History of Muslim Philisophy* (Delhi: Low Price Publications, 1999).

Agai, Bekim, 'The Religious Impact of Science in the Writings of Bediüzzaman' in *Fifth International Symposium on Bediüzzaman Said Nursi: The Qur'anic View of Man, According to the Risale-i Nur* (Istanbul: Sözler Publications, 2000).

Ahmed, Feroz, *The Turkish Experiment in Democracy* (London: Hurst & Co., 1977).

Albayrak, Sadik, *Son Devrin Islam Akademisi: Dar-ul Hikmet-il Islamiye* (Istanbul: Yeni Aşya Yayinlari, 1973).

Algar, Hamid, 'Said Nursi and the Risale-i Nur: An Aspect of Islam in Contemporary Turkey' in K. Ahmad and Z. I. Ansari (eds.), *Islamic Perspectives: Studies in Honour of Sayyid Abu l-Ala Mawdudi* (Leicester: Islamic Foundation, 1979).

Allen, Douglas, *Myth and Religion in Mircea Eliade* (London: Routledge, 2002).

Ashrati Sulayman, 'Said Nursi and the Qur'an' in *A Contemporary Approach Towards Understanding the Qur'an: The*

Example of Risale-i Nur (Istanbul: Sözler Publications, 2000).

Ashur, Husayn, 'Bediüzzaman's Defence Strategy against the Naturalists.' Paper presented at the Symposium on Reconstruction of Islamic Thought in the Twentieth Century and Bediüzzaman Said Nursi, Istanbul, 1992.

Aksam Gazetesi: 'Tarikatçilar' , 7 May 1935.

Aksam Gazetesi: 'Mürteci Bir Seyh ve on Bes Müridi Tutuldu', 5 May 1935.

Aksam Gazetesi: 'Iki Yil Sibirya'da Esir Kalan Said Nursî, Ruslara Düsman Olmustu', 24 March 1960.

Aydüz, Davud, 'Guidance and Teblig in the Risale-i Nur' in *Third International Symposium on Bediüzzaman Said Nursi: The Reconstruction of Islamic Thought in the Twentieth Century and Bediüzzaman Said Nursi* (Istanbul: Sözler Publications, 1995), 188–209.

Basar, Alaadin, 'A Lifelong Principle: Positive Action' in *The Third International Symposium on Bediüzzaman Said Nursi* (Istanbul: Sözler Publications, 1995), 147–58.

Beki, Niyazi, 'The Qur'an and its Method of Guidance' in *A Contemporary Approach Towards Understanding the Qur'an: The Example of the Risale-i Nur* (Istanbul: Sözler Publications, 1998), 92–132.

Bolay, Süleyman Hayri, 'Bediüzzaman's View of Philosophy' in *The Third International Symposium on Bediüzzaman Said Nursi* (Istanbul: Sözler Publications, 1995), 252–80.

Brooklyn College Core Curriculum: Section 14: 'World War I and Cultural Anxiety' in *The Shaping of the Modern World* (2003) at <www.academic.brooklyn.cuny.edu/history/virtual/core4-14.htm>

Bruinessen, *Agha, Shaikh and State. The Social and Political Structures of Kurdistan* (London: Zed Books Ltd, 1992).

Burckhardt, Titus, 'Traditional Cosmology and Modern Science' in Titus Burckhardt, *Mirror of the Intellect: Essays on Traditional Science and Sacred Art* (Louisville: Fons Vitae, 2002), 13–77.

Çelik, Hüseyin, 'Bediüzzaman Said Nursi and the Ideal of Islamic Unity' in *The Third International Symposium on Bediüzzaman Said Nursi* (Istanbul: Sözler Publications, 1995), 247–62.

Chittick, William C. 'Ibn ʿArabī' in S. Hossein Nasr and Oliver Leaman (eds.), *History of Islamic Philosophy* (Islamabad, Pakistan: Routledge, 2001), 497–510.

Dar, B. A., ' ʿAbd al-Qādir Jilānī and Shihāb al-Dīn Suhrawardī' in M. M. Sharif (ed.), *A History of Muslim Philisophy* (Delhi, India: Low Price Publications, 1999), 349–72.

Davutoğlu, 'Bediüzzaman and the Politics of the 20th Century Islamic World' in *The Third Third International Symposium on Bediüzzaman Said Nursi* (Istanbul: Sözler Publications, 1995), 286–311.

Dilek, Şener, 'The Risale-i Nur's Method and Aim' in *The Third International Symposium on Bediüzzaman Said Nursi* (Istanbul: Sözler Publications, 1992), 95–112.

Dursun, Davut. 'Bediüzzaman Said Nursi as the Representative of Social Opposition' in *The Third International Symposium on Bediüzzaman Said Nursi* (Istanbul: Sözler Publications, 1995), 311–24.

Eisenstadt, S. N., 'Introduction' in Max Weber, *On Charisma and Institution Building* (Chicago: The University of Chicago Press, 1968).

Fakhry, Majid, *Islamic Occasionalism* (London: George Allen and Unwin, 1958).

Fromm, Erich, *The Sane Society* (London: Routledge and Kegan Paul Ltd., 1956).

Golpinarli, Abdulbaki, *100 Soruda Turkiye'de Mezhepler Ve Tarikatler* (Istanbul: Gercek Yayinevi, 1969).

Gozutok, Ali, *Muslumanlik ve Nurculuk* (Ankara: Altinok Matbaasi, 1971).

Horkuc, Hasan, 'New Muslim Discourses on Pluralism in the Post-modern Age: Nursi on Religious Pluralism and Tolerance', *American Journal of Islamic Social Sciences*, 19/2 (2002), 68–86.

Horkuc, Hasan, 'Said Nursi's Ideal for Human Society: Moral and Social Reform in the Risale-i Nur'. (Unpublished PhD thesis, University of Durham, July 2004).

Ibn al-ʿArabi, *The Bezels of Wisdom (Fusūs al-Ḥikam)* transl. R. W. J. Austin (New York: Paulist Press International, 1980)

Ibrahim Abu-Rabi (ed.), *Islam at the Crossroads: On the Life and Thought of Bediüzzaman Said Nursi* (Albany: SUNY Press, 2003).

Imtiyaz Yusuf, 'Bediüzzaman Said Nursi's Discourse on Belief in Allah: A Study of Texts from Risale-i Nur Collection', *The Muslim World (Special Issue: Said Nursi and the Turkish Experience)*, 89/3–4 (July–October 1999), 336–50.

Jansen, Johannes J. G., *The Neglected Duty: The Creed of Sadat's Assassins and Islamic Resurgence in the Middle East* (New York: Macmillan, 1986).

Kas, Nilüfer, 'Said Nursi, Teşkilati Mahsusa'dandi' ('Said Nursi was an Ottoman Intelligence Agent') (2003) at <www.tempodergisi.com.tr/toplum_politika/01505/>

Kattani, Ali al-, 'Jihad in Bediüzzaman's Thought' in *The Third International Symposium on Bediüzzaman Said Nursi* (Istanbul: Sözler Publications, 1995), 230–43.

Killioğlu, Ismail, 'The Concept of the "I" in the Establishment of Nature in Bediüzzaman's Works from the Point of View of Naturalist Philosophy' in *The Third International Symposium on Bediüzzaman Said Nursi* (Istanbul: Sözler Publications, 1995), 280–9.

Lewis, Bernard, *The Emergence of Modern Turkey* (London: Oxford University Press, 1961).

Mardin, Şerif, 'Bediüzzaman Said Nursi (1873–1960). The Shaping of a Vocation' in J. Davis (ed.), *Religious Organization and Religious Experience* (London: Academic Press, 1982).

Religion and Social Change in Modern Turkey: The Case of Bediüzzaman Said Nursi (Albany: State University of New York Press, 1989).

Turkiyede Din Ve Toplumsal Degisme: Bediüzzaman Said Nursi Olayi (Istanbul: Iletisim Publications, 1992).

Markham, Ian and Ibrahim Ozdemir (eds.), *Globalization, Ethics and Islam: The Case of Bediüzzaman Said Nursi* (Aldershot: Ashgate, 2003).

Mermer, Ali, 'Aspects of Religious Identity: The Nurcu Movement in Turkey' (Unpublished PhD thesis, Durham University, 1985).

Michel, Thomas, SJ, 'Muslim–Christian Dialogue and Cooperation in the Thought of Bediüzzaman Said Nursi', *The Muslim World (Special Issue: Said Nursi and the Turkish Experience)* 89/3–4 (July–October 1999), 325–6.

Mottahedeh, Roy Parviz and Ridwan al-Sayyid, 'The Idea of the Jihad in Islam before the Crusades' in Angeliki E. Laiou and Roy Parviz Mottahedeh (eds.), *The Crusades from the Perspective of Byzantium and the Muslim World* (Washington DC: Dumbarton Oaks Research Library and Collection, 2001).

Narveson, Jan, 'God by Design' in Neil A. Manson (ed.), *God and Design: The Teleological Argument and Modern Science* (London: Routledge, 2003), 88–104.

Nicholson R. A. (transl.), *The 'Kashf al-Mahjūb': the Oldest Persian Treatise on Sufism by al-Hujwiri* (London: Luzac, 1911).

Nursi, Bediüzzaman Said, 'Sualar' in *Kaynakli–Indeksli–Lugatli Risale-i Nur Kulliyatı (The Epistle of Light)*, 834–1158.

'Kastamonu Lahikasi' in *Risale-i Nur Kulliyatı*, 1570–1678.

'Emirdag Lâhikasi –1' in *Risale-i Nur Kulliyatı*, 1678–1808.

'Emirdag Lâhikasi –2' in *Risale-i Nur Kulliyatı*, 1808–1917.

'Divan-i Harb-i Örfi' in *Risale-i Nur Kulliyatı*, 1917–38.
'Münazarat' in *Risale-i Nur Kulliyatı*, 1938–60.
'Mühakemat' in *Risale-i Nur Kulliyatı*, 1984–2040.
'The *Risale-i Nur* and the Outer World' in *Risale-i Nur Kulliyati*, 2233–41.
'Seeds of Reality' in *The Letters* (Istanbul: Sözler Publications, 1997).
Letters 1928–1932 (Istanbul: Sözler Publications, 1994).
The Damascus Sermon, transl. Şükran Vahide (Istanbul: Sözler Publications, 1996).
The Flashes (Istanbul: Sözler Publications, 1995).
The Flashes Collection (Istanbul: Sözler Publications, 2000).
The Letters, transl. Şukran Vahide (Istanbul: Sözler Publications, 2nd revised edn., 1997).
The Rays, transl. Şukran Vahide (Istanbul: Sözler Publications, 1998).
The Staff of Moses (Sözler Publications: Istanbul, 2002).
The Words, transl. Şukran Vahide (Istanbul: Sözler Publications, 2002).
Nur'un Ilk Kapısı (Istanbul: Sözler Yayinevi, 1977).
'Risale-i Nur'un Te'lif Tarihleri' in *Risale-i Nur 1.0 CD* (Istanbul: Yeni Nesil, 2000).
Tarihce-i Hayat. in *Kaynakli- Indeksli-Lugatli Risale-i Nur Kulliyatı*, (Istanbul: Nesil Basim Yayin, 1996), 2110–2242.

Qummi, Abbas (ed.), *Kulliyāt-i Mafātīḥ al-Jinān*: *Supplication of Kumay* (Tehran: Gulī Publications, n.d.)

Renard, John, '*al-Jihād al-Akbar*: Notes on a Theme in Islamic Spirituality', *Muslim World* 78 (1988): 225–42.

Riker, Stephen, 'al-Ghazali on Necessary Causality', *The Monist* 79/3: 315–24.

Şahiner, *Bilinmeyen Taraflariyla Bediüzzaman Said Nursi (Kronolojik Hayatı)* (Istanbul: Yeni Nesil, 1998).

al-Şayih, Ahmad Abdurrahim, 'The "Bediüzzaman Factor" in the Strengthening of Belief' in *International Symposium: The Reconstruction of Islamic Thought in the Twentieth Century and Bediüzzaman Said Nursi* (Istanbul: Sözler Publications, 1992).

Shabistari, Muhammad Mujtahid, *Dīn wa āzādī* (Tehran: Tarh-i Naw Publications, 1999).

Shermer, Michael, 'The Shamans of Scientism', *Scientific American* (June 2002), 35.

Tasdemir, Mikail, 'Political Thought of Bediüzzaman Said Nursi' (Unpublished MA dissertation, The International Institute of Islamic Thought and Civilization (ISTAC), March, 1999).

Toprak, Binnaz *Islam and Political Development in Turkey* (Leiden: E. J. Brill, 1981).

Turner, Colin, *Islam without Allah? The Rise of Religious Externalism in Safavid Iran* (Curzon Press, 2000).

Tyan, Emile, 'Djihād', *EI*[2] art.

Ubayd, Muhammed Rushdi, 'Methods of Teaching in the Risale-i Nur' in *International Symposium: The Reconstruction of Islamic Thought in the Twentieth Century and Bediüzzaman Said Nursi* (Istanbul: Sözler, 1992), 250–5.

Vahide, Şükran, 'Jihad in the Modern Age: Bediüzzaman's Interpretation of Jihad' in *The Third International Symposium on Bediüzzaman Said Nursi* (Istanbul: Sözler Publications, 1995), 122–47.

'The Book of the Universe: Its Place and Development in Bediüzzaman's Thought' in *A Contemporary Approach Towards Understanding the Qur'an: The Example of Risale-i Nur* (Istanbul: Sözler Publications, 2000), 466–87.

Islam in Modern Turkey: An Intellectual Biography of Bediüzzaman Said Nursi (Albany: SUNY Press, 2005).

'The Life and Times of Bediüzzaman Said Nursi', in *The Muslim World (Special Issue: Said Nursi and the Turkish Experi-ence)* 89 (1999), 208–45.

The Author of the Risale-i Nur: Bediüzzaman Said Nursi. (Istanbul: Sözler Publications, 1992).

Voll, John O., 'Renewal and Reformation in the Mid-Twentieth Century: Bediüzzaman Said Nursi and Religion in the 1950s' in *The Muslim World (Special Issue: Said Nursi and the Turkish Experience)* 89 (1999), 245–60.

Yavuz, Hakan M., 'Print-based Islamic Discourse and Modernity: The Nur Movement' in *The Third International Symposium on Bediüzzaman Said Nursi* (Istanbul: Sözler Publications, 1995), 324–51.

'The Sufi Conception of Jihad: The Case of Said Nursi'. Paper presented at the Peace, Jihad and Conflict Resolution Conference, Georgetown University, Washington DC (November 2002) at <www.iiit.org/iiit seminar/AMSS%20IIIT%20ISESCO%20Seminar.htm>

'Towards an Islamic Liberalism: The Nurcu Movement and Fethullah Gülen', *The Middle East Journal* 53/4 (Autumn 1999).

Index